Once Upon a Midwest Sunset

Stories from the "Nooks and Crannies" Collection

DeAnn Kruempel

Once Upon a Midwest Sunset
First published in United States by BookStudio
2741 Kraft Lane, Missouri Valley, Iowa 51555

Text Copyright © DeAnn Kruempel 2021
Cover images by DeAnn Kruempel, Dorothy Holter, Barbara Magill, Aaron Holter.
Text and layout by BookStudio

Paperback ISBN: 978-1-952891-06-9

Books by the Author

Promises to Keep
Promises Challenged
Promises Strengthened
Promises in Courage
Promises Under Fire

Once Upon a Midwest Sunset

Dedicated to my brother Donald Wolkow. He remembered more than any of
us, maybe because he was quiet and just
listened. I have wished so many times
that I could ask him a question about the
memories in the Nooks and Crannies of
his mind.

The essays in *Once Upon a Midwest Sunset*

appeared in three Midwest newspapers in the "Nooks and Crannies"

column in 2020-2021. I hope that they bring back special memories

and, even better, make you smile.

----dk

Table of Contents

And They Used What?

I don't ever remember having to do without toilet paper. Actually, I don't remember a time when my family did not have indoor plumbing. The youngest of six, the time I came along was the perfect time to come along. My idea of bringing in the cows and using the little outdoor "facility" behind the house was totally different than the attitude of my siblings. I thought it was all great fun. Why? Because I never HAD to experience it. When that privy door clunked shut behind me, (I can still hear the sound.) that was where this five-year-old kid wanted to be.

Ours was fresh, new and state of the art! A cement foundation covered everything that needed covering. The small building had bright white siding and shingles on the roof. Inside was not just a two-holer, there was a two-seater! On the right was a much shorter seat. Goldilocks would have given her stamp of approval— "Just right!"

Hinged covers concealed what, umm, needed concealing. These smooth wooden boards were quite pleasant, only a hindrance when one was in an extreme hurry. There must have been small windows up at the top. I am not sure, because I never looked up, but how else could it have been so bright and cheerful? I could sit on the cover of the Goldilocks seat and read the Sears, Roebuck catalog that lay right next to it. I am sure it was for reading.

Photo by Herman Petersen.

For what other purpose would a catalog be in an outhouse?

One bright, sunny day my mom was hanging clothes out on the lines that ran a few yards away from the outhouse. A perfect time for some catalog reading! Door clunked. Goldilocks would have been proud, but then I found something new on top of the Sears, Roebuck. Pink tissue papers, the ones that mom's canning peaches were wrapped in before she canned them. Little squares of pink that smelled like – peaches! Why were they here in my novelty reading room?

I grabbed one and headed out the door (clunk) to get Mom's take on the peach papers.

They say ignorance is bliss. Well, I was shocked! I could understand how that soft peachy tissue might be repurposed. But, the catalog? All I know is I did not spend as much time "reading" any more. Never again did I see the Sears, Roebuck catalog in the same light.

My next enlightenment on the subject of outhouses occurred several months later at a friend's grandmother's house. This time the visit to the little building was a necessity. The weathered door creaked as I tried to pull it shut. I trembled at the thought of the wind whipping it open. My eyes adjusted to the darkness that was slit into strips by the light that peeked in through the gaping cracks in the walls.

There was a choice of three holes of ascending size. Between the two smaller holes was a nearly-empty roll of toilet paper. Bracing myself with both hands, I managed to pull my body up, legs dangling, on the high seat over the smallest opening. Suddenly, a gust of wind pushed through the opening on the door, tipping the nearly-empty roll of toilet paper. I watched in helpless horror as it rolled over and disappeared into the next hole. Frantically, I searched the mottled darkness for an extra roll. There was none. No peach tissues. No Sears, Roebuck. Wait! What was that down in the corner next to my feet? A small metal bucket filled with—corn cobs?

Holding It Together

A recent tour of my favorite department store revealed a multitude of empty shelves. Mother Hubbard would have empathized. The entire wall that had nestled soft, white packages of toilet paper was bare. There were three lonely cans of bean-with-bacon left in the soup aisle. Considering the shortage of toilet paper, it is understandable that people decided this was not the time to add fiber to their diets.

Born long after the Great Depression, I don't remember having to do without much of anything, but I have been told that in the past Americans have had to deal with severe shortages. World War II was a time when the people on the home front sacrificed for the soldiers doing battle. Tires, sugar, meat and butter were a few of the items that were rationed. "Make it last, make do, or do without" became the motto, and as a nation we stepped up to the plate.

I am certain some of the shortages made life difficult, but it is true that necessity is the mother of invention, and even in the most devastating times in life, there is humor to be found.

Tanks, battleships, and wiring demanded tons of rubber. Before the war the substance was imported mostly from Southeast Asia and supply was adequate, but the bombing of Pearl Harbor changed that and the need became desperate. People turned in extra tires and old galoshes to government collection centers. Driving was limited while tires were recapped, patched and worn down to treads. At that time synthetic rubber was only a gleam in inventors' eyes.

Mabel, Ida, Alice, Anna, Emma, Lilly, Maxine, Julia (Mom, her sisters and friends)

Stretch the old imagination and consider all the other things that were made with rubber-- like elastic. At that time fashion was forefront for many women and tiny waists were in vogue. Women bragged about being able to span their waistlines with their hands and meet thumb-to-thumb, pinky-to-pinky. In their dreams! In order to accomplish such a feat, certain gizmos were required. Corsets and girdles. So, during WWII, American women especially felt the pinch. Clothing

11

manufacturers substituted whale bones for the elastic in those cinch-up devices. Women found other ways to hold up their garments, especially underwear.

Long after this period in history females fondly reminisced, likely proud of their part in winning the war. My mom had four sisters, and all had survived hard times. All were experts at doing without. I was fascinated with their stories, and on the rare occasions when they were together, I stuck around to listen. One Sunday afternoon they were all gathered around our kitchen table.

Mom set the coffee pot on a hot pad in the middle of the women and pulled up a chair. With a smirk, she glanced at Julia. "Do you remember when we wore bloomers?" Julia shot back a warning look, but then smiled.

I did not even know what bloomers were, but I pulled in a chair, too, ready to hear the tale.

Bloomers were an extra set of underwear, kind of poofy, made of cotton. They were fastened at the waist and at the bottom of each leg, which ended just below the knee, with elastic. It seems that the elastic in Julia's bloomers had reached its limit of stretches, so, being the smart, innovative girl she was, she used a safety pin to run a string through the waistband. As long as the string stayed tied in the front, all was well.

One winter day Julia, Lilly and little sister, Emma rode to town with Dad. He dropped them off at the store and went to the elevator to pick up a bucket of molasses. The twins, Julia and Lilly, had orders from Ma to purchase the groceries on the list. Lilly took Emma's hand and started for the coffee shelf.

Julia headed for the barrels of dry goods to find the navy beans. Just as she bent to remove the cover from a container, she felt a slight draft of cold air puff under her skirt. Her bloomers had fallen to the floor in a heap! Like any girl, her first instinct was to look around quickly to see if anyone had seen. Relieved that no men were about, she stepped out of those bloomers, snatched them up and shoved them inside her coat. Suddenly, Julia heard a child's giggle from the next aisle. Emma knew!

Lips pursed to keep from laughing, Lilly rushed through the remaining shopping. Julia did her best to help, though she was somewhat handicapped keeping her left arm clenched against the bloomers.

Twenty years later, five sisters in Mabel's kitchen remembered. Emma started to giggle as she looked across at Julia. "If you could have seen the look on your face!" Lilly broke out in laughter, as though she had kept it in all that time. Ida looked at Mabel and they chuckled. Julia began laughing and soon her whole body shook. The ailment was obviously contagious. Tears streamed down five pairs of eyes as I stared at my mom and my aunts.

At the time, as a young girl, I just figured they were silly old ladies, having a good time, drinking coffee on a Sunday gathering. Looking back now I think they just needed to laugh.

The Original Social Media

It has been said that history repeats itself, but in the case of technology the old is almost always left behind, replaced by the new. When I hear the words "tweet" and "chat" the picture conjured in my mind is of cardinals, finches and sparrows squabbling at the birdfeeder just outside my living room window. My grandchildren roll their eyes or smile tolerantly, knowing that my technology skills equate with the Stone Age. Little do they know that their grandma enjoyed being part of a social media that rivaled present-day telecommunication.

The medium was the same, a telephone, though today's young people would hardly recognize the early versions. Ours was shiny black, big and heavy and rested permanently on a small cabinet in the kitchen. A cord emerged from the back and disappeared into a hole in the wall, eventually connecting to the telephone pole at the end of the driveway.

A rotary dial with ten holes begged fingers to rotate the circle to the stopper. Each hole corresponded with a digit from one through nine and the numbers and letters were clearly marked in a larger circle surrounding the dial. The last hole, the longest turn, was zero, which dialed the operator, a real person! I can still hear the purring sound of that dial as it rotated for each number, then returned to its original position.

The receiver was connected to the base with a coiled line that stretched a couple feet to reach the user's ear. Long conversations required pulling up a chair. The earpiece and mouthpiece were shaped like solid bells and joined together with a sleek, smooth handgrip which fit perfectly in a sort of saddle at the top. Lifting the receiver from its holder gave access to the line, emitting a dial tone or other interesting sounds. Placing the receiver onto its holder pushed down the switch, thus ending the call. The base housed two bells that made the ringer.

What media did this monolithic machine use, which allowed a group of people to connect on the same app? The Party Line! Sounds like fun, doesn't it?

Party Lines were common during the 1950s and 60s, especially in rural areas. Phone customers were linked together with a loop circuit. Each party had their own "ring," which was a mix of long and short rings. You had to know your own code so you could answer the calls coming in for you. Ours was two "longs." Families quickly learned the ring codes of their neighbors, also. If someone else on your Party Line was on the phone you could hear their conversation when you picked up your phone. To eavesdrop or not to eavesdrop, that was the question. The answer was that the whole world became aware of entire phone conversations within twenty minutes. Privacy laws did not hinder social communication on Party Lines.

As a teenager the Party Line social experience was fun and frustrating, depending on whether you were already part of the party or you were outside, wanting in. I can remember being dropped off by the school bus, walking in the front door and heading for the phone. I had to call Nila. After all, it had been nearly 45 minutes since I had seen her. I picked up the phone off the holder hoping for dial tone. Instead, I heard voices. I groaned inwardly and placed the phone back on the "hook." Ten minutes to change clothes, grab a glass of milk and a cookie and I strode back to the phone. The same voices droned on. I listened a bit longer this time. Knowing who is on the line makes all the difference. Great! This woman could go on forever. I sighed heavily into the mouthpiece and waited. Possibly knowing someone was listening in would shorten their conversation. No such luck! Five minutes later I placed the phone back on its rest none too gently. A bit more time passed and I picked up the receiver again. This time I became so engrossed in the conversation that I forgot about Nila until I heard someone open the front door. Mom! She did not approve of listening in, though I do remember an occasion or two when I walked in the room, she gave me the "Quiet" signal, and sheepishly set the phone back in its place.

Then there were the times when I was engaged in a serious conversation with a friend and suddenly we heard the unmistakable click of someone else coming on the line. Discussing the critical issues of teenage life when you know someone is listening just does not happen. Long periods of silence ensued, that is, silence interspersed with three people breathing. At last, the intruder gave up so we could carry on. Not for long. This time the clicking turned to an annoying rattle. Obviously, the person was pushing the receiver button on and off. Then the dialing noise growled through the line. How could anyone be so rude? We responded with another bout of breathy silence. At last, an irate male voice invaded our silent communication: "Will you girls please hang up? I need to make a call and this is an emergency."

Reluctantly, we said resentful goodbyes and hung up.

I waited about a minute and then oh-so-gently picked up the receiver. After all, if this was truly an emergency I needed to know. Mom would want to know, too, in case she had to bake a cake for a funeral or something. The guy had some nerve! He called the Erwin elevator to order a load of pig feed! The idea that he interrupted our meaningful conversation and claimed there was an emergency was appalling. I took great pleasure in slamming the phone down on the cradle!

Most Party Lines were phased out in the 1970s and replaced by private lines, marking the end of an entertaining era. Goodbye to the satisfaction of the dramatic slamming of the phone. Goodbye to the frustration of not being able to get on the line because someone was already on it. Chats and Tweets are fun, I am sure, and the whole world will still know your business in minutes, but can anything compare to the original social media? HellO-O! Why do you think it was called a Party Line?

Stir Crazy!

Consider for a moment the cooking tools used in American kitchens over the past few generations. My great-grandmother, who began housekeeping in a sod house on the South Dakota prairie, probably owned a wooden spoon, a few large bowls, a fry pan, a kettle and a baking pan. As time went on, gadgets were invented to make life easier, so Grandma's cupboards and drawers included a wider range of utensils including a wooden spoon, probably a gift from her mother, a selection of bowls, kettles, pans, a tea kettle, cookie sheets, bread pans and more. Married just after the Great Depression, my parents started out with much less. No cupboards or drawers in their little farm house; I remember Mom telling me that their kitchen furniture consisted solely of peach crates. But Mom had a sturdy wooden spoon and bowls and a few wedding gifts that she treasured. Farming was good during those years and, combined with a work ethic that wouldn't quit and the introduction of electricity to rural America, Mom's kitchen soon embraced a plethora of work-saving devices. She worked alongside Dad in the fields, raised a passel of kids and fed their family. I remember her spending long periods of time in front of the stove, next to the table, or in front of the kitchen sink with the trusty wooden spoon in her left hand, stirring. Soups, puddings, cakes, frosting, fudge, rolls, tuffies, everything made with love to share with her children and grandchildren.

The meals-in-minutes microwave and instant pot have since claimed the places of honor in modern day kitchens. Mom's recipes that required stirring constantly for ten minutes were filed in the back of the recipe box long ago. Then the recipe box became obsolete because it was quicker and easier to find a recipe online. In a very short time, our cooking styles (and lives) changed drastically. "From scratch" steeped to "quick," which simmered to "instant." Housewives and househusbands wanted meals in a hurry. All at once there was little need for a wooden spoon. Cold, hard metal and mundane plastic spoons replaced the comforting wooden tool, the one that held the memories.

In the midst of the present pandemic, our society has been suddenly forced to make a drastic shift from a frenzied attempt to fit everything into crazy work and play schedules to simply staying home. Youngsters have packets to complete and online classes to view. Parents are learning more than they ever wanted to know about teaching their child at home but were afraid to ask. For the first time, maybe ever, people have time on their hands. Stir Crazy!

Posts on social media endeavor to make light of the situation. Children have been quoted as announcing, "I hope I don't have the same teacher next year!" One cartoon depicts visitors looking in on a family of quiet, focused children. The mother explains, "I told them the glue sticks were lip balm." Then there is the photo of the ancient-looking woman with deep wrinkles, gray, straggly hair, and dull, lifeless eyes. The caption reads, "This is Jane, age 33, after 4 hours of homeschooling her children."

Some families are using the time to the best advantage. Beautiful paintings are gracing refrigerators that never would have been created had we not experienced this isolation. Beads, ribbon and fabric are being shipped to homes everywhere. Very young children are exhibiting artistic talents that have grown out of encouragement from Mom and Dad who suddenly have time.

In the kitchen, cobwebs have been swept from the oven. A new trend is taking over the country—the "what-was-left-in-the-freezer" cuisine. The result has been not only an interesting blend of flavors, but also an exciting realization that cooking can be fun and rewarding. A month ago, how many times did we totally depend on the microwave to get us a quick and easy meal? Patience ran thin after even three minutes of waiting. After a pandemic-induced U-Turn, families are asking, "What do we do now?"

Old cookbooks have been pulled from the shelf and dusted off. Even Grandma's beloved recipes that were put on the back burner because they took too long to prepare are reappearing. So is the wooden spoon! Mom's had a thick, sturdy handle. The bowl part was stained to almost black and smoother than the handle, as though all those timbery cells had been sealed tight. The best part was that after close to seventy years of circling clockwise through every dough and batter, soup and sauce, that spoon had become a lefty. The bottom quarter was worn down to a perfect angle for scraping the bottom of a pan.

When Mom had to go to the nursing home and her illustrious days of cooking were over, my sister, also a southpaw, claimed the spoon. So far, she has added another twelve years of mileage to that stirring device, mixing up favorites, often to share with her children and grandchildren. Last week she set a covered bowl out on the front step. The grandkids who stopped to pick it up smiled and thanked her as much as social distancing allowed and called to her, "You make the best chili ever, Grandma."

She has told them the story, so they flashed a knowing grin when she replied, "It's the spoon." Then she waved and turned back to her kitchen with the left-handed spoon and said in her heart, "Thanks, Mom."

MOM'S BROWN SUGAR ICING

1 cup brown sugar
½ cup white sugar
1/3 cup half & half
4 Tablespoons butter
1 Tablespoon white corn syrup
¼ teaspoon salt
1 teaspoon vanilla

Put all ingredients except vanilla in medium sauce pan and bring to a rolling boil. Stirring constantly, boil 1 ½ minutes. Remove from stove. Stir while cooling. As it begins to thicken, add the vanilla. Continue stirring until it reaches frosting consistency. Spoon on 9 x 9 cake and spread quickly. (Mom's note to me: "I have real good luck with this recipe. If I'm in a hurry I put the pan in cold water, then it gets stiff much faster, but you must beat it all the time while in cold water.")

(My note to readers: For best results use an old wooden spoon!)

Revive the Drive

Life has flipped a U-turn for many Americans in the last few weeks. Suddenly people discover they have time they have never had before but with far fewer opportunities for which to use it. Social gatherings are restricted. Parks and recreation areas are closed. In spite of the limitations, families are honing their social distancing skills to perfection, making the best of the challenging situation.

People are still connecting, often with amazingly creative means. Revive the drive! Cars, buses and SUVs are steering people together, not too close, but close enough to show they care. A little girl in our small town recently celebrated her fourth birthday. The child was devastated that she could not have the usual party with friends and Grandmas and Grandpas, games, cake and ice cream, but her parents put an idea in action and soon the child was enthralled with a new and unique entertainment. From her car seat in the family mini-van, the little girl, her sisters and parents saw evidence of a caring community. From hundreds of windows Teddy Bears smiled and waved, often holding balloons or cards with special messages. Someday, her parents will tell her the story of her traveling birthday back in 2020.

Then there was the woman who recently turned 90. For the past year her children and grandchildren had planned a huge gathering to celebrate the milestone birthday. Well, COVID-19 put a brake on that, but extraordinary circumstances led to extraordinary measures. On her special day her children encouraged their mother to come out to the front step and enjoy the sunshine. Soon a familiar car drove by slowly with a colorful banner extended from the open window. Within seconds, more cars came and people called out good wishes. A whole caravan of nearly forty vehicles paraded by to extend birthday wishes. The unexpected surprise contributed by a multitude of well-wishers made the birthday one to remember.

In a nearby community, buses led a procession of vehicles around school bus routes. Teachers and support staff drove through city streets and country roads to connect with their students and encourage them to carry on with their studies in spite of the quarantine. Routines and roles shifted, and face-to-face communication yielded to honks and waves and smiles.

More and more folks are buckling up and heading down the road. A new appreciation has emerged for sunsets. Flowers and trees seem to have suddenly appeared in landscapes, when in reality, they have been there all along but unnoticed until now. There are places to go, sights to see and always, lessons to be learned.

Back up nearly sixty years to a Sunday afternoon on the farm where I grew up in eastern South Dakota. "Dinner" dishes were done and Dad ambled into the kitchen. "Want to go for a drive?" He addressed Mom, but my ears perked up. Sunday drives were a fascinating mix of family history, animal science, agronomy and juicy tidbits of gossip about people who lived long before I was born. I don't remember Mom ever turning down the offer. In five minutes, we headed down the driveway in the '59 Ford Fairlane 500.

No cell phones back then. No GPS navigation devices. Why would there be a need for such things? If we got lost, Dad knew which direction he needed to go, and there was no worry that we would soon be back on track. The small wing windows between the windshield and the glass on the driver's and passenger's side were cracked open, the air conditioner of that time.

The spring had been a dry one, but some of the crops were peeking through. "Look! You can row the corn already." Dad was proud of his crops, especially his characteristically straight corn rows. Mom smiled, knowing that the drives were his way of affirming his farming skills. Always, it was fun to compare the neighbors' crops.

The country roads were narrow, claiming two smooth wheel tracks with a loose gravel row down the middle and mounds of coarse rock on both sides trailing down into the grassy steep ditch. Fortunately, the chances of meeting another vehicle or being tailgated were slim on a Sunday afternoon.

With his crops still in view, Dad's head veered to the right and so did the car. Suddenly there was a crunch of tires wobbling over loose gravel and we could feel a slight pull toward the ditch. Mom's right hand instinctively reached for the small chrome handle on the vent window. "Don't go in the ditch!" she said as she shot a glance at Dad. He just grinned, put the car in park and assured us he would be right back. We watched as he stopped at the barbed wire fence, lifted the top wire up and pushed the second down, then bent over and stepped between them. Out in the field, he reached in his pocket and pulled out his pliers. Opening it wide, he used one of the handles to dig down into the earth right next to a hill of corn. Then he made a quick visual inspection of the area and soon the car door slammed shut, and we were back on the road again. Mom looked at him expectantly, for she knew he was worried that the crops would suffer from lack of rain. The severe drought they had experienced growing up had to lurk in the back of their minds.

"There's still moisture about four inches down." My farmer dad sounded hopeful as we continued on the journey. A pattern usually ensued at this point, with a trek through his old stomping grounds, then to where Mom grew up and her brothers still farmed, but each drive presented different points of interest. A pair of ducks bobbed in a shallow pond, part of a slough that had nearly dried up. I asked my father what kind they were. "Probably mud hens. You don't see many ducks or geese any more. Too dry this year." Then we cruised by an empty feedlot, and my parents talked about the brothers who had owned and lost it.

We were approaching my mom's old neighborhood. She pointed to a wooded area where stark black trunks pointed to the clear blue sky. "Remember there was an orchard there? We used to go and pick apricots." I tried to imagine lovely green trees loaded with blossoms, but the dead trees stifled my vision. Dad turned down an unfamiliar road and I peered out my window, curious about what might be on this new route.

It seemed like we drove on forever, but it was probably just a few miles. Here and there people were out in their front yards and sent us friendly waves, but many of the places were empty, their families having moved to the city. Mom pointed to one abandoned farmhouse and recalled how she worked there one summer. Her mother had helped the woman when she lost a baby. Fields and farms slid by, and the countryside seemed more desolate with even fewer houses.

A sod-covered approach came into view that led to a road, rather a two-wheeled path. There were signs on both sides of the narrow lane, "Low maintenance road" and "Enter at Your Own Risk." Much to Mom's dismay (and my excitement), Dad swung the Ford down that road, and we swerved and dipped along. Mom shot her husband that "Are you out of your mind?" look as her hand again reached for the security of the vent window handle. Dad's eyes met mine via the rear-view mirror, and I caught the familiar twinkle and the smirk on his face.

"I remember the old Beckner place out here. There was a brick silo and a huge white barn. My brothers and I brought the horses and wagon over on the Fourth of July. If there were enough of us, we had a baseball game,"

Father reminisced as we floundered a bit farther. "I think it was just over the hill…"

Between us and the hill the road dipped abruptly. In that short dent a pool of water was standing, daring us to take a dive. Mom quickly sat up straighter, looking around as if to find a good place to turn around.

The next thing we knew, Dad accelerated and charged ahead, straight into the murky pond! By this time Mom's knuckles gleamed white as they clung desperately to the vent knob, and I figured her right foot had pushed clear through the floorboard.

No doubt we would have made it, but there was a hollow lurking in the depths where water had gnawed away the earth. The right tire dropped in deep. Mom's side. Mud flew as the wheels spun. The driver tried forward, then a quick shift to reverse, unknowingly applying the principle of inertia. The hole held on. We were stuck.

Dad blew out a deep breath and turned to Ma. "How far is it to John and Willa's?"

Mom stared straight ahead and we could feel the tension stretching as tight as a rope. "Half a mile," she snapped icily. Not another word escaped her, but the message was as clear as glass. "I told you so."

He opened the door and carefully placed one tall work boot down into the mud. Then the other. With a hand on his car, my dad paused just for a second, looked in my window and winked. Then he lumbered back up the road less traveled.

Yes, even then, long ago and far away, there were places to go, sights to see and always, lessons to be learned.

Uphill Both Ways

"Well, back in my day…"

Grandpa begins to reminisce about his school days when a teenage grandson cuts in. "Yes, we know, Grandpa. You walked ten miles to school every day, uphill both ways." The classic dialog has grown to tradition in the Over the River and Through the Woods location. The grandchildren roll their eyes with a tolerant grin. Grandpa nods with sage wisdom. Though he admits to slight exaggeration, there is a message he hopes to convey to the younger generations: Life was not easy at that time.

I started first grade in public school, but my three older siblings and my parents did walk to school every day. Their walks were more than a mile, but many young people had to trek two miles or more. Country schools were common in rural America into the 1950s. Often called "one room schoolhouses," the structures accommodated one large classroom in which every student, grades one through twelve, studied the three Rs.

Winter presented unique challenges for the teacher and students. The teacher needed to get to school early to start the heater. Frigid temperatures

Rose Hill School #12 Last Day of School Picnic at the De Smet Park.
(Deloris Gilbertson)

and deep snow drifts made the long walk close to impossible some days. The stove in the center of the room warmed those in the closest desks, but students near the windows and walls often needed to remain bundled in coats and boots. Coal or wood was hauled in from the pile outside, a job for the older boys. Youngsters took turns bringing canisters of water for drinking and washing.

Everyone brought their lunch, often carried in repurposed tin pails, and during hard times some lunches were meager, consisting of a slice of bread and maybe a wrinkled apple. In all but the most severe weather the youngsters hurried outside for noon break and two recesses. All that fresh air and communing with nature had its advantages and fascinating outcomes. A former school teacher who taught in a country school in Iowa told me about one of her students who grew exceptionally fidgety one day after recess, wiggling and squirming and shuffling his feet. He jumped up right during class and began stomping and shouting. Suddenly, there was a soft thump and a small garter snake landed on the floor and, tongue flitting, slithered toward the teacher's desk.

The infamous outhouse stood outside the building, the only restroom available, offering one side for girls and one for boys. Children did not dawdle or make frequent requests to use the "necessary," at least not in cold weather.

Always there are stories to be told, and sometimes the tales did not come together until later, like the one about the smoke in the outhouse. Writing paper was a luxury and at one particular country school a youngster dejectedly reported to the teacher that a sheet had been ripped out of her precious notebook, leaving a jagged tear. The next day when the students filed in following noon break it was reported that there was smoke coming from the hole in the boys' side of the outhouse. That night Johnny's mom noticed that his hair seemed uneven and smelled as if it had been singed. After a moment of hesitation, he replied to his mother's concerned inquiry that it had happened at school when he "lit the fire." Assuming that he was referring to lighting the stove, she admonished her son to be more careful in the future and thought no more of the incident.

Several weeks later, Johnny's little sister, who was just old enough to pay attention to the talk on the playground, asked her daddy at the supper table, "Pa, is it true that if you wrap leaves up in paper and light a match to them, you can smoke them, just like cigarettes?" Hmmmm. Obviously, smoking in the boys' room originated long before flushing!

Many former scholars from one-room schools look back on their education with fond memories. Older students helped the little ones, often learning in the process. The youngest worked independently while the older students were having their lessons, enabling many to learn above grade. There was a sense of community and a caring comradery that could only exist where everyone worked together in close proximity.

Today, because of the COVID-19 quarantine, students are again working together in close proximity. A fifteen-year-old boy does school work in the same room as his twelve-year-old brother and little sister, age six. Mom and Dad are doing their best to make lesson plans for each level and assist in the learning process. Some families engage in distance learning, using computers and iPads. They read books and prepare reports. The older kids help the youngest. Squabbles ensue. Enlightening adventures in culture and art transpire around the kitchen table. Children are learning life skills that reinforce math, science and language. Last week the engineering lesson requirement was to go outside and play in the snow. Sleds were dug out. Forts and snowmen arose from the whiteness. Snowballs flew. Albert Einstein would have approved.

In forty years, today's young person will probably reminisce as they sit at the dinner table with their grandchildren. "It wasn't easy back when I was a kid. Why, one year we all had to stay home for months. There were no school activities or sports, and we couldn't go see our friends or even go out for french fries. If we didn't do what we were supposed to, we got grounded from the PS4. We had to have school at home. Mom and Dad were our teachers, but they liked my little sister best. I had to listen to her read, and I had to help my little brother with multiplication. For lessons we did cooking and cleaning. It was tough back then in 2020."

☼

Playing in the Dirt

Long before the Coronavirus Pandemic infested our world like an invasive species, researchers lauded the advantages of communing with nature, scratching in the soil. Besides the obvious benefits of growing food and flowers, they listed increased physical activity, lower stress levels, and an influx of vitamin D. Some scientists still maintain that working outside in the dirt can strengthen the immune system, especially in children. If you have ever seen the look of pure pleasure on a child's face as they jump into a puddle and watch the water fly, you know the most valuable benefit; it is just plain fun.

Having dabbled with growing things since I was knee high to a grasshopper, the garden calls my name as soon as the temperatures hover over the freezing mark. Most years I am stocked with plants and seeds, but two weeks ago I decided to place an order with my favorite nursery only to unearth the fact that they were not accepting any orders. Their stock was depleted. They could not keep up. For whatever reasons, American families are playing in the dirt!

Digging back a few years, though not privy to today's recommendations from health professionals, my parents definitely knew the value of outside play. There was a sandbox next to the front yard fence. My brother, who at the age of four took farming very seriously, decided he needed to work outside the box. He claimed the six by ten-foot patch next to the sandbox as his own, and soon it became a delightful pile of loose dirt. He spent hours there every warm day, plowing, disking, dragging and planting. Delmer smiles as he remembers one day when Dad stopped to watch. With "putt-putt" noises resonating from his lips, the boy scooped windrows of sand, grass and dirt into his John Deere trailer and hauled them to the tiny green elevator. He turned the crank and the belt conveyed the "grain" up and into a peach crate, my brother's "grain bin."

I can see the crinkles at the corners of my father's eyes as he proudly observed his little boy, imitating himself. Finally, he cleared his throat. "Well, son, it looks like you are busy with your farming, and you are doing a good job of it." Delmer kept working, his heart swelled with pride at the praise. "I'm headed out to plant corn. Do you think you have time to come and ride with me on the John Deere 520, or do you have too much work to do?"

To this day my brother marvels at the fact that Dad considered the child's play so important that he gave him the choice of continuing his own farming or riding on the tractor in the field.

My older sisters still reminisce of the hours spent outside, growing up on our South Dakota farm. They had cleared an area out in the woods where they had a "play house." Tree stumps, wooden boxes and old boards served as tables and chairs and an oven. Mom contributed old pots and pans, so the girls enjoyed days of play in their secluded spot that was surrounded by brush, trees and weeds. One of their favorite earthy activities was making mud pies.

Dirt was plentiful and they mixed it with water from the cattle tank. The crates made good ovens, and soon delectable pies were stashed in a tin pail, ready for serving to our supportive family. One day Dorothy and Darlene were stirring up their pie ingredients when they decided they should add some plant materials. After all, Mom and Dad said to eat our vegetables; think how pretty those mud pies would be, embellished with bright green flecks! So they foraged the area for the prettiest green leaves available. They pulled them from the tall stalks, brought them back to their playhouse kitchen, and tore them up into the mix. A few hours later both sisters were plagued with burning, itchy welts all over their hands, arms and legs. It turned out that their garnishing greens came from the stinging nettle patch!

It could be the girls passed their experience down to their younger sister because this girl's Mud Baking 101 class took place within the fences of our yard. My stove was an old sawhorse. It even had a bent nail that turned, making the perfect temperature control. I liked to think of my concoctions as cookies rather than pies. I even used a stick to scrape orange powder from a soft brick onto the tops. After all, presentation is everything. Martha would have been proud! After baking the little circles in the sun for a day or two, it was time to seek adult approval.

Stacking the mud cookies onto the shiny lid of a paint can, I carried them and a few empty walnut shells to the front stoop and waited. Usually, Mom was the first one to come along and was invited for tea. In her apron and homemade cotton dress she would sit next to me. "Your cookies look delicious," she would say as she smiled and took a pretend nibble. "Mmmm, sugar cookies, my favorite!" At that moment I resolved to make even better mud cookies next time. Then she slurped loudly from the tiny nut shell, her pinky finger lifted daintily.

I don't ever remember Mom or Dad saying they were too busy to test our mud pies or encourage our ground level enterprises. They took the time. Back then they were not concerned with stress reduction or vitamin D intake or strong immune systems. They just knew how very important it was to simply have fun.

☼

What We Remember

Isn't it amazing how different people remember different things, whether it be about a long-ago incident or something that happened "only yesterday"? Sometimes I think we choose what we remember, maybe subconsciously.

Last week a vehicle pulled up to the front of the library for curbside checkout. The windows rolled down. A woman was in the driver's seat and her two young sons sat in the back with a cardboard container between them. Each child rested a hand on the box that was perforated with small holes. One of the boys called out, "We got baby chicks! Do you want to see them?"

Of course, I had to decline. Social distancing was required, but in my mind I could definitely see those soft, downy wonders.

First grade was definitely not my favorite time of life! On my third day, I decided school was over-rated. Oh, sure, it was good to learn to read about Dick and Jane and Puff, but the students in my rural South Dakota school grew up on farms, and we all had our own Puffs and Spots, so after a few weeks we already knew the words and hoped for a bit more excitement in the stories. At recess the big kids got to do all the fun stuff. So, every night when I went home I told Mom about the day and the disappointments. She listened, which was enough to fortify me to go back the next day. After all, that is what one does.

One cold day in late February, I got off the bus and headed into the kitchen. Mom was nowhere to be found, but there was a note in the middle of the metal table: "I am at the brooder house."

I rushed upstairs to change into my everyday clothes, pulled on my chore coat and boots and trudged through the snow drifts down to the small white building that was built for one purpose. Before I even got to the door, I could hear them. There was a cacophony of peeps and cheeps, baby chick chatter!

I knocked softly on the door and Mom opened it with a warm smile on her face. She did not have to caution me to be quiet. I remembered. The door shut with a click and instantly every chick stopped in place, poked its head up, and held its breath! Several seconds elapsed while 51 pairs of little dark eyes stared, waited. All at once, one chick decided I was not the In-credible Hawk and turned her head down to peck at something on the floor. Almost instantly every other small ball of fluff relaxed and began to move about---and peep. We slowly stepped to the straw bales that she and Dad had lined up to make a smaller area. Then we sat and watched.

Three heat lamps hung from the ceiling, all placed near the center of the contained area. Mom had taken apart the cardboard boxes, the shipping car-tons, and spread them out on the floor. The shredded bedding that came with them was layered on the cardboard. There was a distinctive medicine-like scent that mixed with straw and feed, which I can smell as I write this. The lamps warmed the small structure, and sitting there next to my mom observing the antics of the most adorable creatures on earth was heaven to a five-year-old.

The heat and light sources were strategically placed. One was close to waterers, which were mason jars nestled upside down into red plastic dishes. Though only one day old, the tiny creatures ventured to the water, dipped in their beaks and lifted their heads to swallow. All at once a bubble floated to the top of the jar with a "blurp!" Again, the flock assumed their alarm position.

One lamp dangled near a long, galvanized trough of chick feed that had a turning bar on top. I asked Mom what the bar was for. She explained that it kept the chicks from crawling into the feed, scratching it out, or pooping in it. As we whispered, some of the little critters pecked at the crumbles. Meanwhile, twenty others assumed it was recess time and they tore across the cardboard, making little pattery noises with their chick-feet. We chuck-led quietly.

At last, I could wait no longer. "Can I hold one?" Mom's gentle gaze skirted her precious brood. She found one with a little black splotch next to its eye. Very carefully she stepped over a bale and scooped up the baby. She waited for a few seconds until all the chicks had calmed, then gently placed her in my hands. I am pretty sure at that moment I became the Crazy Chicken Lady.

The little chick poked her head up, but as I stroked it with my index finger, she soon snuggled down and closed her eyes, thinking, "Are you my mother?"

In the warmth of one of the lamps one downy creature settled down onto the soft bedding and tucked her beak under one wing. She was soon joined by seven others, cuddled together, content with life. Nap time.

Mom and I perched on the bales in that brooder house for at least an hour. Little did I know then that sixty years later I would treasure the time and remember it so vividly. I hope that someday the two little boys with the baby chicks have memories as special as mine.

Where's the Fish?

The crappies are biting in area lakes! This spring more people are enjoying the water, picnicking, hiking and fishing. Across the nation there has been an increase in the number of fishing licenses sold. No surprise. The age-old activity lends naturally to social distancing. Fisherman's code requires setting up a good distance from another angler; tangled lines are best avoided. The lure is strong and for some, 2020 may be remembered as the year they had time to get hooked on fishing.

Interestingly, I have discovered that "Hook, line and sinker," most great fishing memories are not about the Big One that got away. Many do not even involve fish!

My niece affectionately described her first contact with a rod and reel in a college writing class. Her family had moved far away from friends and the home she loved. At age six, Kim was downright unhappy. When her dad proposed a fishing excursion to the nearby lake, the girl cast away her worries. They strolled hand-in-hand, pulling the child's little red wagon loaded with tackle and a cooler full of snacks. At the lake her father taught her how to tie the proper knots and bait the hook. Her first attempt at casting reeled in a nearby bush, but patience paid off and soon the child sat happily next to her father, their bobbers gently riding the waves. To this day, Kim fondly speaks of her first fishing experience, "I didn't catch a fish that day, but it didn't matter. It was an unforgettable time, just Dad and me."

It is natural for people who enjoy certain pastimes to want to pass on that gratification to their children and grandchildren. My mom loved to fish! When grandchildren visited, they were often treated to a few hours at the lake. Our girls often reminisce about the time they spent, and smile when they relate that they made Grandpa put the worm on the hook. One daughter always insisted that they throw the fish back. She also remembers the wild horses that grazed near the shore.

Before they had grandchildren our parents valued family time, and fishing was a priority. There were six of us kids and our family excursions were often quick trips after a heavy rain postponed work in the fields. One spring day Dad decided we would go to Big Stone Lake. It didn't take Mom long to have kids, clothes, tackle, food and fry pan packed and ready to go, and we were off. After two-and-a-half hours on the road, we checked into a cabin while Dad went to rent a boat. No boats allowed on the lake that day! The infamous South Dakota wind was stirring up waves that crashed into the shore with ocean-like breakers. Seven sad faces and a crowded cabin inspired Dad to inquire at the office, "Any other fishing spots nearby?"

Minutes later we were on the road again, our destination was Nine Mile Lake. Maybe it was the trees surrounding the water, maybe it was divine intervention, but for some reason the wind was not a problem at Nine Mile. The family had to take turns going out in the boat, but each cruise was rewarded with a great catch of perch. Mom knew just how to fry them. In spite of the change of plans, the story had a happy ending.

Then there was ice fishing. I can hear the smile in my brother's voice as he tells of the time he stopped at the frozen lake when, driving by, he saw Mom and Dad's car. As he walked out on the icebound expanse, he immediately spotted a small red pool on the ice between the two fishermen. Bundled in warm layers, the couple sat contentedly, each on a five-gallon pail turned upside down. They welcomed their son while keeping one eye on the small cork bobbers in the perfectly round fishing holes. Delmer stared at the red pool, obviously concerned. Mother grinned and pulled off her insulated mitten. Dad's handkerchief was wrapped around her index finger, showing a dark spot where blood had seeped through.

The tale revealed that the five-pound northern she had pulled from the lake had caught Mom's finger with a razor-sharp tooth when she was removing the hook from its mouth. She nodded proudly at the fish that lay close to the car, tail still flapping. Just then the cork disappeared into the icy water in the hole in front of her. She jumped up and reached for the short wooden pole.

A little blood was not enough to stop our mom. Not when she was fishing!

Fire Up!

Is there any aroma more tantalizing than that of homemade bread, fresh from the oven? The cinnamon-spice scent of warm apple pie could take a close second. During this stay-at-home time people have swept the cobwebs out of their ovens and enjoyed the delicious rewards of their labors. Social media posts report of youngsters' baking assignments for the week. Pie crust and bread top the list. Yeast has replaced toilet paper as the item in short supply at the grocery store.

Growing up in rural South Dakota, homemade was the standard. Bread, cakes, cookies and pies decked our kitchen table every day, bubbled, browned and baked in the cook stove in the corner. Mom's stove sported white enamel on the front and black cast-iron on the cooking surface. Cut-out circles formed the burners, with a notched hole near the edge. A special metal handle fit precisely into the notch for lifting the burner. To make heat under each burner and in the oven, fuel had to be added; the ubiquitous corncob came through again!

Two immense piles of corncobs huddled right next to the corn crib north of the barn, the leftovers from a visit by Claus the corn sheller. We kids kept the wooden box next to the stove loaded with cobs. My siblings all remember filling buckets and bushel baskets and hauling them from the pile to the kitchen, often in our Radio Flyer wagon.

Adding more cobs, or a small chunk of wood increased the temperature. "Preheat oven to 350 degrees" translated back then to "add 20 dry cobs, three medium sticks of wood and wait ten minutes." To test for the Goldilocks requirement, Mom opened the oven door part way, reached her hand in, palm down, and turned it slowly, feeling the temperature. The handy hand thermostat registered just right. Her precious cook stove browned almost everything to perfection. On baking day, four loaves of bread cooled under a flour sack towel following a slathering of butter. Some kind of pie, depending on the orchard or the freezer bounty at the time, adorned Sunday dinner dessert plates. The cookie jar did not disappoint. At Christmas time, we baked lefse directly on top of the stove. I remember wiping off the browned flour with a rag, quickly enough not to get burned, but not so fast that flour flew everywhere.

Every wonderful invention has its drawbacks and the cook stove presented no exception; some were downright scary. The smoke from the burning fuel vented outside through a shiny, black metal pipe that extended up from the back to the brick-lined chimney above. Weeks and months of burning added layers of soot and creosote as they ascended toward the outside sky. Unfortunately, these caked-on substances sometimes caught on fire.

One weekday afternoon, Dad drove to De Smet to pick up some shingle nails at the lumber yard. Mom whipped together the ingredients for angel food cake batter and fired up the stove. Angel food required a high baking temperature at the beginning and throughout the entire hour of baking time to keep the cake from falling. As she waited for the oven to preheat, an unusual odor permeated the air, something burning mixed with the smell of scorching metal. Her eyes traveled up the stove pipes to discover that their normal black color had flared to bright red just below the ceiling. A fire raged in the chimney! Chimney fires easily spread to the dry wood that surrounded the cinder block. As a result, many homes burned to the ground.

Our mother sent us outside with orders to stay far away from the house. Somehow, she managed to reach Dad by phone. He probably came close to blowing out the engine on the old Ford '59 pickup as he raced to get home. Jumping from the truck, our father took a mental roll call of the family and then scanned the roof. The chimney puffed black smoke, and translucent waves of heat swirled out in waves from the surface. The boys ran with him to get the ladder from the Quonset. Mom and the older girls carried pails of water from the cattle tank. Our stomachs clenched with fear as we watched Dad climb the ladder, a bucket in his right hand. As quickly as possible, he hauled up pail after pail and sluiced the roof around the chimney. Finally, the furious flood of smoke diminished to a trickle.

The folks' eyes met. Mom's brows still creased with worry when Dad ventured into the house. From outside we heard him testing the pipes. At last, satisfied that the house was safe, he called us back inside.

The story had a happy ending, but it branded our family's thoughts for a long time. Life experiences change one's perspective. We no longer took the fire in the cook stove for granted or all the delights it brought forth. Even the heels of bread loaves melted in our mouths. Apple pie filling bubbled through the top slits with spicy goodness. Chocolate chip cookies came out perfectly crisp on the edges and just the right chewiness on the inside.

But it was a long time before Mom baked another angel food cake!

Murky Waters

"Do I HAVE to take a bath? But, I'm not dirty!"

The age-old objection to soap and water has befuddled parents of every generation. Manufacturers responded to their pleas for help with an array of products designed to entice bathers. Today, children revel for hours in a tub chin-full of colored bubbles. Wind-up boats paddle through the waves. Big-toothed sharks squirt water at sparkling crystal faucets that gush perfectly warmed water on demand.

Float back in time to the not-so-distant past. In rural America, from 1900 to the early 1950s, before electricity and indoor plumbing, bathing involved a far more complicated process. The Saturday night bath! Why on Saturday, you ask? The cliché "Cleanliness is next to Godliness" held water; for whatever reasons smelling good on Sunday was a priority.

If the thought of a weekly, rather than daily, dip causes your nose to twitch at the imagined stench, also known as body odor, consider the work that family hygiene demanded back then.

Bath water needed to be heated, of course, so no matter the time of year, my older sisters stoked the trusty old cook stove with a few handfuls of corncobs and several small chunks of wood the brothers had split. Our family was fortunate enough to have a water source inside the house, the pump in the corner. We younger kids pumped frigid water into pots and pans, and Mom hauled them to the stove, covering every possible inch of the cast-iron surface. Saturday night required gallons of hot water!

While the kettles heated to boiling, my sister Deloris brought in the tub from the porch and placed it close to the stove. Ours was oblong, made of galvanized metal, and sported sturdy flip-up metal handles on two sides, while some were round and some fashioned of copper. An old rug awaited splashes as the bathers stepped out in our kitchen. Two rough, sun-dried, white towels hung over a wooden chair that stood close by. A bar of white Ivory soap nestled in a plate on the seat.

Back to the pump, kids! This time we filled buckets and poured them directly into the tub. Dad grabbed potholders or dish towels and ordered the kids to stay back while he carried the heavy kettles from the stove and cautiously added the boiling water. Mom's hand swished through the water to assure the Goldilocks temperature, and more cold or hot was trickled in accordingly.

Research and family memories differ as to the traditional bath order. Some remember Dad diving in first. Others say in their family the oldest girls sloshed while the water was still hot. Regardless, one must first contemplate the restrictive size of the tub. There was no way an adult or a nearly full-grown adolescent could stretch out their legs, say nothing of managing a comfortable sitting position. No, simply lowering one's body into the water challenged a contortionist. Tall people assumed unique yoga positions like the Knees Squash Nose pose. The Hokey Pokey was invented! You put your left foot in, you put your left foot out….

Each member of the family took their turn, whether in ascending or descending order. At our house, the folks and the older siblings were given private bath time while everyone else waited in the living room. Mom knelt by the tub, wash rag in hand, as the younger ones bathed. I never understood why it was so important to "scrub behind your ears." I do remember our mother saying the dirt was growing in back there, so obviously I had failed on that account.

The Ivory floated which saved time (and soap). Though the water was not deep, by the sixth person, murky replaced crystal clear, and the temperature crept into the glacial range. No one wasted time in the tub, especially the final bathers.

At last, when scrubbed faces shone and freshly clothed bodies smelled squeaky-clean, Dad and my oldest brother Donald grabbed the metal handles and hauled the quagmire outside. Mom's petunias in the front yard thanked them in summer. In winter they dumped the water into the nearest snow drift. I was the youngest, the sixth child, but I don't remember being "the baby that was thrown out with the bath water."

Bath night was different back in the day. Time, water and soap were all used sparingly. Nothing was wasted. Soaking in hot luxurious bubbles was not an option. Rubber duckies would have quacked in dismay, wind-up toys ground to a halt, propellers stuck between knees and tub.

We may have all bemoaned Saturday bath night; I don't remember. Like most things back then it required hard work, but the weekly ritual was part of life. We splashed, scrubbed and shampooed once a week---whether we needed it or not.

☼

Bovine Intervention

Tails waving in the air, young calves frolic through the pasture as their mothers stand by, contentedly chewing their cuds. A cow bends to sniff her baby as it lies curled up, hiding in the grasses. The idyllic scene often greets the observant on leisurely spring drives down country roads. Every cattle farmer will agree that the journey to such a pastoral setting was not an easy one; rewards intertwined with toil and heartbreak.

Graze back in time a few decades when nearly every farm in the Midwest kept some type of livestock. The sound of playful calf bellows pervaded the summer air when we grew up on our eastern South Dakota farm.

Farm animals gave birth in the spring. That was the plan, but it is not nice to fool Mother Nature! Many a farmer trudged through a blinding March blizzard, seeking the calf that came early. Later, seeing the pools of mud in the yards was almost a guarantee that there would be at least one new delivery. Dad and my brothers occasionally needed to wade through muck over their boots to rescue a newborn and carry it to the barn, followed by the bawling, anxious mother.

In every animal species there are those with personality, and even the toughest of farmers grow attached. Cows often become overly protective of their new offspring, so as a child I was seldom allowed inside the barn fence. We had one cow that was very tame and gentle, and every year, without fail, she produced two healthy calves. Twinny loved to have her head scratched and Dad never worried that she would harm us, even when she had babies.

One late April afternoon, Don informed Dad that Twinny was about to calf. Dad nodded and smiled, undoubtedly picturing the matched pair soon to appear, happily nudging their mother for nourishment.

The chore time check revealed that this spring was different. The beloved cow was having trouble. Dad sent me to the house. "Have Mom call the vet." Twenty minutes later, Doc barreled into the driveway. I followed him through the gate and pulled it shut behind me. Dad gave me "the look" and pointed out.

Sorely disappointed, I moped out of the shed, but I worried about Twinny and was determined to see her new babies. My father didn't say I could not watch; he simply indicated I was not to be in the cow yard. Sneaking around the granary I knelt by the fence on the south side of the pen. Undetected, I could peek between the boards.

It seemed like forever, but finally I saw a dark red form squirming on the ground. I released a sigh of relief. One little calf. Settling back in, I waited. And waited. Where was the next one?

The precious cow was not getting up to lick her newborn in the age-old ritual of nature. I angled my head between the boards to get a better look and Dad spotted the movement. Busted! I watched as he looked down, shaking his head. Then he slowly walked to me as I stood on the other side of the fence, waiting.

Eyes filled with tears, my strong farmer dad told me that we lost Twinny. He hesitated for a few seconds, then looked back at the scene behind him. Don and Delmer were rubbing the new calf with a gunny sack. After a few minutes it struggled to stand; finally, on wobbly legs the creature began its search for mother.

Dad motioned to the boys and they carried the wrapped bundle to us. The calf was the tiniest I had ever seen. I watched in amazement as it slipped under the fence and floundered into me. "Do you think you can take care of it?" Dad asked. The small creature bawled pathetically, and the white head turned up with big, brown imploring eyes.

Tiny and I grew up together that summer.

Unlike Twinny, most bovines turned rather testy when they gave birth. We had one roan cow that took it upon herself to protect all of the youngsters, whether hers or not. More than once the guys scurried frantically to the fence to avoid her charge, shaggy head swinging as she careened after them. Known as "Mean Cow," everyone avoided the critter like the plague.

The men hauled feed and hay with the tractor and loader until spring grasses grew and the cows and calves could go to the big pasture. Two tractor tires stacked on top of each other made a perfect hay feeder. One cold March Day, with bales piled on the loader, Delmer discovered something interesting in the tire feeder. Four legs flailed in the air. A large, shabby head twisted back and forth, crying pitifully in distress. Mean Cow was trapped in the feeder, upside down!

Possibly karma came to mind as the men remembered the wild eyes rushing at them, but they lifted one of the tires and worked together to turn the animal over. Once on her feet, she turned back to stare at the guys before galloping back to her fellow bovines. Amazingly, after her rescue, Mean Cow was never mean again.

Growing up on a farm, many animals journeyed through our lives. They had unique personalities; we rescued, cared for and loved them, and mourned when they were gone. We made their lives the best we could, and they changed ours forever.

Moody Broody Revisited

To a very small child life is full of possibilities and there is no limit to the imagination. Each day provides an exciting new adventure until, well---life hatches. As a young child I idolized my parents and five older siblings, especially Mom and three sisters. Totally fascinated with their exploits, I longed for the day I would be old enough to do the same.

I remember skipping outside to find Mom doing the chicken chores. She lugged pails of feed to the coop. "Can I help?" I asked as my small hand grabbed a handle, likely hindering more than helping. She smiled and we trudged on. I followed her to the cattle tank where she dipped out a full bucket of cold water, carried it in her left hand, her right arm lifted.

We entered the building. Some of the flock remained inside and greeted Mom with soft chicken chatter. Bars of bright sunlight beamed to the floor from the south windows. Tiny dust motes swirled through the light, magically shimmering in faint rainbow colors. Hens jumped to the feeders and pecked happily.

Time to gather eggs. In anticipation, Mom turned to the rows of metal nesting boxes that lined the east wall. A large circle opening in every compartment welcomed the layers. Yellow oat straw lined each nest. She gently placed the white ovals in her bucket; two or three easily fit in her work-worn hands. The container quickly filled, and Mom smiled at the bounty.

A white hen remained in the last box in the bottom row. She clucked softly as we neared. Mom explained to me that this was a broody hen, a cluck she called it; she wanted to set on eggs and raise chicks. Without hesitation, Mom reached under the hen and withdrew three white treasures. The hen fussed a bit and pecked at Mom's hand, then fluffed her feathers and settled back down.

I gazed at the snowy-white gems in the bucket. A contented smile covered my mother's face. I could not wait to get big enough to take care of the chickens!

Time passed slowly, but finally, my opportunity arrived. A note on the table from Mom: "DeAnn, please do the chicken chores. I will be home before supper." Yes! Anticipating the fun of this new experience, I quickly snatched the galvanized pails in the porch and headed for the granary. It took two trips, but I hauled the corn, oats, and ground feed. These waited outside the coop while I hurried to the water tank. Right arm lifted for balance, I carried the sloshing bucket of water with my left.

I hopped into the henhouse. Startled birds flew around wildly, trying to escape the intruder. Dust roiled in the air, settling on my face and arms.

With feeders and water trough full, it was time for the fun part, picking the eggs! Bucket in hand, I turned excitedly to the nests.

Six beady eyes of huge, winged creatures glared at me. As I neared, one of the broodies puffed the feathers on her neck and emitted a throaty growl. She clucked loudly and tucked her eggs under her with a sharp, scary beak.

Sweat broke out on my forehead. Tentatively, I stretched my hand toward the nest. A fowl snarl split the air and that biddy pecked me! Ouch! Immediately, I checked for blood. A purple bruise began spreading ominously. I glanced with dread at the other two, hunkered down, ready to attack.

There had to be another way. I tucked the bucket under the nests and scurried outside. There on the ground lay the perfect answer to my dilemma, a stick! Back inside I approached the boxes, bravery ebbing with each step. The cluck fluffed up even bigger and lifted her head, daring me to try. With hand as far back as possible, I pushed the stick toward her. She attacked it like a hornet, but I managed to reach under and pull out one egg. My heart pounded. I began to think that Colonel Sanders had the right idea.

That chicken and I had a stare-down, and I am pretty sure she won. Finally, I reached in as fast as I could, grabbed her by the feathers on her back and pulled her, kicking and screaming, out of the nest. Hell hath no fury like a chicken scorned! With an angry screech, that girl flew the coop, clucking noises echoing.

I had done it! At last, I could get to those eggs without suffering irreparable injury. I looked down. There on the floor were two white shells, split open, oozing yellow liquid.

Somehow I managed to gather the remaining eggs that day, but after that, dread replaced anticipation whenever I had to do the chores.

Years later, I sat next to Mom as she admired the ceramic hen our family brought her. She asked how my chickens were doing, and I suddenly felt that I should confess the times I was not kind to her hens. I opened my mouth to speak, but she beat me to it. With a knowing smirk and blue eyes twinkling, she shook her head, "When I was a kid, I hated chicken chores. There were always those big, old clucks in the nest. They were mean."

She looked down at her hands as she remembered, and I wondered if she had used a stick. I wondered if she had checked for blood.

☼

Through the Wringer

Monday--wash. Tuesday--iron. As we grew up in rural South Dakota in the Fifties and Sixties, Mom adhered to the daily chore traditions whenever possible. Before automatic clothes washers and dryers, doing the family laundry required planning and physical labor.

Monday mornings we often found our mother sorting dirty clothes into small piles on the kitchen floor. The assemblage began with whites and graduated to light colors, brights, darks and finally jeans and overalls, the order matching the degree of grime.

Once batches were determined, Mom tugged her revered Maytag washer from its resting place in front of the window in the porch and positioned it in the middle of the narrow room. Directly behind the washer she placed a sturdy wooden bench which held the galvanized tub for the rinse water. An old chair sat next to the rinse tub. There the vinyl-lined apple basket waited for the clean, squeezed-out laundry.

The washer was a large metal tub on four legs with wheels. Above sat the wringer which consisted of two hard, black rubber rollers housed in a dome that swiveled 360 degrees. A flexible drainage hose extended from the bottom of the tub and hooked onto the upper side. On top of the roller housing, a propeller-like bar twisted on an axis to loosen or tighten the rollers. A metal shield extended above them which could release the roller tension if a bulky item got stuck. A lever on the upper left side set the rollers turning either forward or reverse. Extending the same flat trigger away from the machine unlocked the wringer unit, allowing it to turn in a complete circle to enable wringing over vessels all around it. A small red button, the agitator switch, protruded from the front.

Hardware in place, Mom began the process of hauling water buckets. It took several trips from the kitchen sink to fill the washer tub with hot water. The hinged cover on top remained open until the tub was full. Mother then filled the rinse tub with cold water.

She dumped a measure of white powder into the open machine, closed the cover and pulled out the red agitator button; hot suds awaited the first load. Our mom preferred the detergent in the big yellow box. She said it kept whitey-tidies bright. For a time she switched to the soap in the red box. Could be the Tide formula suffered a temporary lapse. Could be the whitey-tidies were not so dirty. Whatever the reason our kitchen cupboard soon overflowed with sparkling new tableware. A 22K trimmed plate, cup, saucer or glass with a wheat design came free in each box of Duz detergent.

Mom carried the first load to the washer and let those items agitate a few minutes. After starting the wringer, she fished out the clothes, one item at a time, and carefully placed it between the rollers, which pulled it through while squeezing out excess water. The items plopped into the clear rinse water in the tub on the other side of the machine and waited to be swished around, then run through the wringer again, this time landing in the clothes basket.

When the last pair of dirty overalls had been scrubbed, rinsed and wrung into the basket, Mom unhooked the hose and held it over a bucket to empty the murky water. Wash and rinse water were dumped outside.

When my sisters and I helped, Mom stood by, always with the warning, "Don't get your fingers in the wringer." Over time, hundreds of socks and undies swirled through that old Maytag.

All went well until a stranger attempted wash day. It is ridiculous to consider a cold, hard wash machine anthropomorphic. Such a gadget cannot exhibit human characteristics! We discovered later that Herbie was vengefully loyal to our mother.

One Saturday in late October, Dad got very sick and needed to go to the hospital. Mom was desperate. The only person she could reach who could be there in less than an hour and stay with the kids was Grandpa's eccentric friend who had moved from Chicago. We quickly learned that Horace tolerated no nonsense. His philosophy rang clear: children were to be seen, not heard.

Monday morning as we left for school, Horace was muscling Herbie into washing position, muttering something about "If a woman can do it…." The trouble began, Horace recounted later to Grandpa, when a long white towel wound back around the roller and twisted so badly, he could not find the beginning or end. Growing impatient, he thrust the bottom of a cotton shirt into the washer. As the sleeve approached the rollers, a huge pocket of water squirted out, directly into Horace's glasses. Deciding that was the last wrinkle, the codger roughly engaged the release lever for the roller arm. It spun around and crashed into the porch window! Lightning-like cracks radiated from center to corners.

That night as we sat around the supper table eating silently, a car drove into the yard. Six kids charged outside, thrilled to have Mom and Dad home.

As we headed back to the house, Horace rushed out. Pushing long arms into coat sleeves, he brushed by, strode to his car, fired up the engine and spun out the driveway. He didn't bother to say goodbye or explain the broken window.

That was probably just as well; Dad and Herbie would have put him through the wringer

Much to Do With Nothing

Once upon a time not so long ago there were no iPads or computers. Phones were not particularly smart. A laptop was where you sat when Mom or Dad read books before bedtime. You could write in your tablet, and the best ones were red, and "Big Chief," a Native American in full headdress, looked on proudly. Some evenings the family gathered in front of a screen, a television; black and white pictures flashed weekly episodes. In our home, Dad selected the entertainment for the night, which was not always the kids' choice.

Though electronic technology was limited when I was a child, I do not ever remember being bored. Possibly I mentioned the word once and my mother responded by placing a hoe in my hand and voicing the words, "Good. The potatoes need weeding."

On our South Dakota farm the outdoors beckoned, especially in summer. Trees were particularly appealing and we swung from them, climbed them and cleared areas in them for our play house. We repurposed cans, crates and discarded dishes and pans to create a working kitchen and spent hours stirring up culinary delights from dirt, water and whatever other materials we could scrounge.

In early summer a hunt through the bales in the haymow often revealed baby kittens, much to Mother Cat's dismay. Soon after, the young felines, decked out in dresses and bonnets, bounced along as we pushed them in our navy blue, hooded doll buggy.

When the corncrib was empty, the cement floor invited skating. We dug out the metal skates from the toy box, attached them to our shoes with the skate key and rolled along. Hopscotch numbers lasted a long time in the crib. Limestone rocks wrote almost as well as chalk, then served as "throwers."

A box in the porch overflowed with outside "toys": sand pails and shovels, tractors, bats, gloves, baseballs, softballs. If a sibling was available, we could go to the granary and play Ante I Over. One yelled the words and threw the ball. The other one, with luck, caught it as it came down the other side. Only on a few occasions did the roof hold the ball for ransom.

We tied knots on the ends of a rope cut the right length for jumping. How many jumps could we count until we missed one or dropped to the ground, exhausted? Or silly rhymes held our focus as we jumped with the rhythm: "Cinderella, dressed in yella, went upstairs to kiss a fella. By mistake she kissed a snake…." I smile remembering my mom accepting the jump rope challenge. In her everyday dress and apron, she "skipped rope" and competed with the best of us, easily making one hundred skips.

The old shop smelled of oil, corncobs and mice. As soon as we kids were tall enough to peek above the bench, we discovered a crank hand drill and a vice. The hammer and coffee can of various nails on the side tempted us beyond resistance and resulted in an immediate visit to the wood scrap box. I don't think Dad was too excited about us using his shop, but he always managed a smile when we proudly displayed our lopsided car, bird house or doll bed.

My brother Delmer owned the coolest store-bought pistol and holster. Of course, fighting bad guys required more than one gun, so he traced that pistol on a board and painstakingly cut around it with Dad's coping saw. To the younger sister, the wooden gun he made was far more impressive.

Thomas Edison once said, "To invent, you need a good imagination and a pile of junk." We didn't call it junk back then. Possibly it was a throwback from war times when nothing was wasted, but the folks saved string, boxes, cans, wooden spools, rubber bands and scraps of paper, all of which invited invention.

On cold winter days hours wiled away as we watched our windup coupe scuttle across the kitchen floor. An empty thread spool, a match stick (with the fuel end cut off) for winding, a strong rubber band threaded through the spool hole and a paperclip or button to hold the rubber band, pieced together to make a car. The brothers sometimes notched the spools with a jack knife. Traction was critical!

Spools and plastic measuring cups became tables and chairs in the paper box doll house. We threaded a string into a large button and tied a circle large enough to tug and release between hands. The resulting noise rivaled Crocodile Dundee's frantic SOS signal.

Thick catalogs provided dresses and shoes for paper dolls that we drew and cut out. My sisters designed their own wish books by pasting catalog pictures onto folded sheets of paper. Small fingers spread a gooey mix of flour and water on the back of the pictures; flour paste was the "tie that binds"!

Cylinder oatmeal boxes easily converted to drums and tambourines. Cutting them into doll beds created a quieter entertainment. When Mom needed quiet, we colored. An old cigar box housed hundreds of crayons of every length and color. I honestly believe the same box dispensed those crayons through all six of us kids. Only the cover eventually fell off. Then it became the ramp for the stock truck.

Yes, Mr. Edison would have approved.

Blowing in the Wind

Sunshine, gentle breezes and cool temperatures made the perfect day to hang out laundry, but even if the weather was not ideal, the clothes were hung outside. When I grew up in rural South Dakota our clothes dryer consisted of three wire lines stretched between three T-posts stationed in the back yard. The sun bleached and brightened the towels and shirts. The wind flapped, billowed and dried the sheets. Cool temperatures made the clothes, sheets and later the whole house, smell heavenly.

(Dorothy Holter)

Laundry needed to be dried in winter, too. Sometimes the coveralls froze before we could clamp on the clothespins. Freeze-dried stiff as a board, they made a comical sight when carried in like a dance partner.

The drying display of washing was organized in an orderly fashion, so on summer Mondays dazzling whites all swayed together in the wind. Colors flashed next with unmentionables on the middle line between sheets and towels; some things were best kept hidden! Warm sun rays soaked into heavy dark chore clothes, but the thick seams remained damp for a long time.

My sisters and I all helped hang out laundry. I was not very old when Mom pulled down the heavy metal wire with the sliding clothespin bag so that I could reach in and grab two clothespins and hang up a washcloth. She smiled then and said, "I love to hang out clothes."

Sixty years later, like the flash of light when the sun peeks from behind a cloud, I realize why my mother and generations of other women held dear the vision of their wash flowing gently in the wind; the picture portrays the story of their lives.

Just married and on their own, Mom draped her farmer husband's overalls, work shirts and socks next to her homemade work dresses and aprons. Every day of her life she worked beside the man she loved.

More than a year later the sun blessed tiny pink booties, along with diapers, soakers and kimonos. Mom fondly hung small white sheets on the line between her clothes and Dad's. Months passed and soon blue receiving blankets and little boy rompers joined the other baby clothes as the woman cherished the scene and the new chapter in her life.

Many full clothes baskets later, the overflowing lines danced with dresses, shirts, and pants of every size and color, mingling with nearby diapers and bibs. Mother's gaze swept the scene and proudly accepted the new episode, her growing family.

Later on, patches plastered knees on jeans and overalls, no matter what the age of the man, for farm work was hard; sometimes patches covered patches. Gradually, dresses and shirts faded and wore thin as they were passed on from child to child. Hand-me-downs guarded the meager budget. Did her eyes cloud with worry or weariness as the mended garments whipped before her in the wind?

It did not seem like many wash days later when bright reds and whites flashed between the poles. Jerseys, shirts, sweaters and socks flapped like flags as school sports took the lead. Juggling schedules and farm work challenged the best of parents. The mother's role stretched to include the behind-the-scenes booster club, and life was so full that time flew by.

The pages turned in the mother's story. Soon the mountain of laundry dwindled to a small hill and some of the lines were bare when she scanned them, empty basket at her feet. Everyday dresses and aprons snuggled next to overalls and striped shirts, and again, she worked side-by-side with her farmer. Though some clotheslines were empty, her life was full, and she looked forward to the next chapter.

One Monday morning Mother carried her basket to the line early. Guests slept inside and breakfast cinnamon rolls were rising on the counter. She reached for the tiny pink dress on top and her eyes glistened as she tenderly clipped it to the wire. Little pajamas printed with cars and trucks waited for her loving hands. At the bottom of the hamper lay a small blanket, on which bears and elephants invited snuggling into the blue softness. The corners were worn thin. On the line the coverlet swayed in the breeze.

She heard the front door squeak open and soon a child rounded the corner. A grin of anticipation lit his face and he toddled toward Mom. Suddenly he spied the blanket and reached for it. He plopped to the grass clutching the soft, wet corner and his thumb found his mouth. Content that now all was well in his world, the little boy gazed up at the woman next to him with trusting, blue eyes and breathed "Gram-ma." Her heart melted, and she beamed happily.

Yes, her story was written there week after week, proclaimed by the wash on the line. If we had thought to look, we may have seen it, too, for it was there all along, blowing in the wind.

And There's Pie!

"Come on in and sit up to the table. There's always enough for one more!" The screen door creaked open as Dad ushered in a guest at 11:50 AM. Mom was accustomed to setting an extra plate on the kitchen table for an uninvited visitor. Vacuum cleaner salesmen, guys who sold every kind of brush imaginable and the occasional lost soul searching for "the home place" turned into our drive, often at meal time. Though it happened too often to be a coincidence, our parents welcomed them into our home. Sometimes Mom would pull us aside and whisper, "Don't take very much gravy," or "We will split a pork chop." Somehow, there was enough.

Corncrib side doors.

More than five decades ago, on our farm in eastern South Dakota, the meals were breakfast, dinner and supper. Lunch was the snack in mid-afternoon (and maybe mid-morning) to "tide us over" until supper. Early to rise and strenuous physical labor required energy, and our mother and her four daughters rose to the task; hearty meals graced the table daily.

When the men worked in the fields, planting, cultivating, or harvesting, at four o'clock one of us kids carried a bucket to the fence row and waited for them to drive back to the end. Then we would sit companionably in the grass and munch on the sandwiches and cookies Mom had prepared. Dad enjoyed a thermos of coffee with homemade, gingery molasses cookies. If the lunch bearer was lucky, she was rewarded with a ride on the tractor for a round or two.

When Dad hired builders or painters or any extra help, those men always shared meals with our family for the duration of their jobs. "You have to treat your help right" was our father's philosophy, and Mom accommodated with bountiful fare on the table.

Every year in mid-September, Claus the corn sheller would lug his huge rig to our place and maneuver it next to the corn crib. Neighboring farmers brought trucks and trailers to haul the shelled grain to town or to our empty bins. It was a corn-shelling bee! Dad, my brothers and the neighbors loosened the ears from the bin and pulled them with rakes to the long conveyer. The corn traveled to a short elevator and into the sheller. Golden kernels poured out of an auger into the waiting trucks. Bare red cobs tumbled to a pile near the crib. Husks and cob chaff spewed out of a different tube, everything to be used later.

At noon Dad led the men to the kitchen and an overflowing table. One young farmer stopped in to apologize to Mom. "I promised my wife I'd come home for dinner." The others ribbed him about being newly-married and pressed him to stay and eat. "There's pie," they said just as he spotted the three tins on the counter. He leaned closer and caught a whiff of cinnamon and apple. "I guess I could call her and tell her I won't be coming," he said, and Dad pointed to the phone. In the crowded kitchen, it was impossible for us to avoid hearing his brief conversation. He explained to his bride that he would not be home for dinner, then waited for a few moments as she replied. At last, releasing a frustrated sigh he blurted out, "Maybe you could learn to make pie!" A short stretch of dial tone followed.

The guests sat at the table and began passing the heavily-laden bowls and platters. They filled their plates with sliced roast beef, potatoes and gravy, green beans and creamy coleslaw. Homemade dinner rolls, quickly slathered with butter and chokecherry jelly, teetered on the edge. Seasoned eaters found room for dill and beet pickles.

Mom and her girls listened to the clatter of silverware, bowls and glasses as the crew focused on the food. They jumped to fill serving dishes and coffee cups when the need arose. At last, our mother dished up the grand finale, wedges of crust-covered apples swimming in spicy-sweet filling. Claus and the young farmer reveled in two slices, the latter murmuring that he needed to stock up.

The culinary offerings abounded in our farmhouse kitchen, especially when we had company. The experiences taught us kids about warmth and hospitality, how to treat visitors in our homes. We learned that you need to be good to your help, and truly, there is always enough for one more.

Fair Play

The Fairlane Galaxie 500 lurched slowly over the low curb as Dad maneuvered it into the grassy lot that served as a parking area. The dust-coated grass lay flat in the wheel tracks and footpaths that led to the front gate. The drivers of the other vehicles that filed into the lot that September morning set their sights on the first row to save as many steps as possible. Dad aimed our Fairlane toward a tall ash tree in the middle of the field, then eased it into the shade cast by the golden leaves.

Six noses pressed as close to windows as possible. At last, nearly bursting with excitement, we piled out the doors. We were going to the fair!

The man at the admissions gate stamped our wrists and the adventure began. Rows of farm machinery, dotted with colorful signs and flags, beckoned. Dad and the brothers meandered to the Green section after promising us girls that we would meet back at the front gate at 1:00.

With one hand tightly grasped by an older sister, we followed our mother through the various attractions of the South Dakota State Fair. The Women's Building housed jars of fruits and vegetables and paper plates loaded with cookies and rolls. Spectators explored glass cases of artfully displayed needlework.

Flowers and potted plants created inviting pathways as we wandered through the horticulture building. "Isn't that a beautiful rose!" Mom exclaimed as she pointed at the delicate blossom in the clear vase. We agreed, enthralled at all the beautiful exhibits.

The morning flew by and soon tummies growled. Mom checked her watch and we started back to the front gate where the men waited for us. We ambled to the car, still shielded by the shadow of the ash. Dad opened the trunk and the brothers helped unpack its contents. The older girls spread out two large army blankets. Mom unwrapped the towels and layers of newspaper that covered the blue porcelain roaster. The enticing aroma of the still-warm fried chicken wafted to our noses as the lid jiggled. Peeling layers from a large plastic bowl revealed potato salad, embellished with egg slices and paprika. The fare included homemade dinner rolls, garden tomatoes and apple pie. Years later, we all wondered at our mother and the work she did to provide such a feast for her family's day at the fair.

Picnicking on the wool blankets, we recapped our morning, savoring the food and the moments shared. Wedges of cinnamon-spiced pie slid down easily. Then Mom poured lemonade into plastic glasses and we rested in our shady spot.

Ready to go back, the crew repacked everything into the trunk and trekked again to the front gate. The man checked our stamps and we began the afternoon. All eight of us strolled through more buildings. In the commercial area, businesses displayed their wares. Pens, pencils and balloons lay out on tables, free for the taking. Later, Dad walked with a yardstick in his hand, like a staff clicking lightly on the stone paths.

Scattered throughout were open entertainment areas. Square dancers circled around, bright colored skirts swaying. One man carried a boa constrictor wrapped around his arm and shoulder, asking children if they wished to pet his baby. High school choruses and bands performed on wooden stages. We munched on popcorn, given out free in small red and white bags as we listened, the nearby water fountain adding to the music.

No farm family could resist the animal buildings. Hogs, cattle, horses and sheep called to passers-by. Chickens and geese and every domestic bird imaginable stared at us from metal cages. Row after row of buildings—we visited all of them.

Calliope music and fearful shrieks lured us to the Midway. Vendors waved plastic hats and swords. Tattooed men hawked their games. "Win a Teddy Bear for your girl!" Though we kids were tempted, Dad said the contests were rigged and a waste of money. Men on stilts tottered above us. Girls screamed as the Tilt-a-Whirl twirled by. Mom waved from a bench below while we rocked in the top car of the Ferris wheel. After the rides we plucked tufts of purple cotton candy from the spun sugar spheres Dad purchased for our treat.

The grandstand show for the evening was the rodeo. As we descended the steps to our seats, the cacophony of the announcer, the crowd and the calling peddlers elevated the anticipation while we waited for the event to begin. The cowgirls and cowboys gave quite a show, but my hero was the clown who ducked into a barrel when an angry bull threatened to gouge him with its sharp horns.

In later years, 4-H took the lead and the fair was full of deadlines and preparation. Our parents could boast of children who excelled. Hogs, cattle, chickens, eggs, vegetables, baked goods and demonstrations earned blue and purple ribbons and trophies. Judging contests brought top honors with one sister going on to place in national competition.

We all learned from the experiences, but my favorite fair memories are of when I was little and we went just to have fun. Maybe it was the time spent all together as a family. Maybe it was the picnic in the shade of the ash tree with the best fried chicken on the planet.

What Next?

7:00 AM. A farm truck rumbled into the driveway and disappeared past the barn. Soon a red tractor followed, pulling a grain wagon. The driver jerked back the long clutch lever as Dad and the boys called a greeting, then rammed it back into gear as they all headed for the corn crib. The men cleared a strip next to the building and dragged out rakes and shovels. Soon Claus drove into the yard with his sheller, deftly maneuvered it next to the crib and laid down the chain-run conveyer. Corn Shelling Day was about to begin!

The annual event occupied a fairly short time in farm history in the Midwest--after the invention of the corn picker, but before the incredible combine. In the early 1900's farmers harvested corn by shocking and binding, backbreaking toil. They cut the stalks off at the ground by hand, bound six or eight together and then tied those into larger bundles, forming a tent-like shock. The bundles of stalks waited in the field like trees on a Christmas tree farm as the attached ears of corn dried, later to be loaded onto racks and hauled to barns for winter feed for the livestock. After the Depression and the drought of the Thirties, corn picking machines appeared on farms, making much faster work of the harvest. Tractors pulled the pickers that ripped the husk-covered ears from the stalks and dropped them into the wagon behind. The kernel-loaded cobs were then hauled to corn cribs to dry.

Some cribs were round and made of wire or cribbing. Ours was long and narrow and sided with wooden slats. There were spaces between the thin boards, allowing air to circulate so the corn would dry and not mold. A cement aisle ran down the center of the building with storage rooms on both sides. In the fall before harvesting the new crop, farmers took turns helping neighbors with

The corncrib as it looks today

corn shelling. The huge machine chewed the grain from the cob and conveyed it into trucks and trailers, which then hauled the golden kernels to our bins or to the elevator in town.

Corn shelling was a big event on our farm in South Dakota. Many hands make light work, and several farmers gathered together prattle more than any women I know!

As Dad and one neighbor began to unlatch the top-hinged doors along the side of the crib, my brothers stood next to Claus and two other men and watched. Rex, the stray that stayed, wagged his tail wildly in anticipation. Doors creaked as they were lifted and propped open, and the ears of corn began pouring out onto the conveyer that carried them to the corn sheller. Suddenly the heads on the brome grass near the building fell and lifted, like waves in the ocean. Rats and mice poured out with the corn! All at once one of the men yelped as he jumped from one foot to the other and slapped his overalls just below the knee. The others laughed. "That was quite a jig you just did!" They teased and slapped him on his back. None too happy about having a rat crawl up his bare leg, the young farmer glared at his peers and strode to his truck. He came back with several circles of used, brown baler twine. He cut it with his jackknife and tied it tightly around the bottom of his pants. Though they chuckled at the sight, not one of the fellow workers refused his offer to share the twine.

Rex made quick work of the rodents and soon a pile of bodies lay next to the crib. My brother Delmer remembered pouring food into his bowl that night. The dog sniffed, whined and staggered back to the doghouse.

At noon, Dad invited the workers to the house for a feast prepared by Mom and her four daughters. As we set the table before they came in, she reminisced of the days when she was growing up and helped her mother feed the crew that came to help bind and shock. She said she and her four sisters cooked and baked for three days to have enough food for the twenty hungry men.

After letting their dinner settle, our shellers went back to work. When the last ears were pulled out with rakes and shovels and the last golden kernels poured out of the auger, three mountains of dry red cobs stood, ready to be hauled to the shed. My brothers began sweeping the cement floors in the empty crib, and the helpers leaned against the corn sheller, resting in the shade. Dad seldom bought beer, but on this special day, as a treat for the workers, he brought out six-packs of Hamm's and Pabst Blue Ribbon.

The men sat for a spell, reveling in camaraderie and after-work-is-done banter. They reflected on how much easier their lives were now, since the Old Days. One man wondered how their folks had ever managed without working themselves into an early grave. Claus' gaze swept from his corn sheller to the wagons and trucks and rested on the corn crib. He heaved a great sigh and nodded his head thoughtfully. "What will they think of next?"

Food for the Soul

Just-picked-and-shelled peas and new potatoes for supper! No need to worry about us eating our vegetables with a menu like that. We youngsters looked forward to summer fare that included all the fresh produce we could eat from our South Dakota farm garden.

Every spring Dad hooked the John Deere 520 onto the retired rusty farm disc that rested under the trees at the edge of the small field. A few rounds and the loosened soil was ready to produce another batch of vegetables for the family.

Mom taught us at a very young age how to hoe between the rows and pull the weeds. The carrots had to be replanted more than once when one of us confused their feathery little tops with those of some invasive scourge. We learned how and when to pick beans, then helped cut or snap them into pieces ready to be cooked in the pressure canner. Ours held just four quart jars and sported large black wing nuts that fastened the cover down tightly. Though the device made her a bit nervous, Mom was glad to have it and told us how before the days of pressure canners, her mother boiled jars of vegetables for hours to can them. We helped prepare beans, corn and carrots. Every bit of extra produce was squirreled away for winter use.

By midsummer the northwest corner of the garden gleamed with color— Mom's flower garden! Red, white and peach-colored gladiola spires reached for the heavens in the back rows. Cannas with red tops towered next, creating a striking backdrop for the dahlias, cosmos, asters, sweet peas and zinnias. Moss roses cushioned the paths with a flower-splotched green carpet. Four-o-clocks flashed pink and yellow trumpets every afternoon, true to their name. Peonies, roses and petunias nestled in beds around the house, inviting a walk-about.

Every Saturday evening, our mother marched out the front door, scissors in hand. Twenty minutes later, she returned with an apron full of cut flowers and a smile on her face. Lovely bouquets graced our kitchen table, especially on Sundays, displayed in vases she treasured, gifts from her sisters or mother or our dad. The arrangements held the place of honor, displayed on a delicate crocheted doily she or one of her sisters had made.

All that beauty in her flower garden was meant to be shared. Like Hermes, the FTD messenger, Mom showed up with a bouquet in her hands when visiting a neighbor or members of her family.

Many seasons passed. Summer gardens grew, produced their bounty, and winter turned the plants into soil for the next year. I had my own family, my own garden, far away from home. Mom visited, and I could not wait to show her my garden, lush with rows of beans, peas, carrots and potatoes. She gazed over the expanse and I waited for her song of praise. Finally, she spoke. "Where are the flowers?"

I felt a pang of disappointment, for I thought of all people my mother would surely understand. "I need to raise as much food as I can, Mom," I explained, picturing the jars stashed in our pantry, my contribution to feeding the family.

Moments passed in silence and at last I glanced over to my mother. Her face was lifted up to the sky where the sun's golden rays framed a huge puffy cloud. Crinkles deepened next to her eyes as she turned to me. Wisdom reflected in those blue eyes, lessons learned from years of life lived to its fullest and hardships overcome. Softly she said, "Flowers are food for the soul."

Today, more than thirty-five years later, I sit at my dining room table. Before me a single rose brightens the room, nestled in an etched-glass vase that belonged to my mother. The precious, round white doily underneath enhances the centerpiece. I gently stroke the outer pink petal, a layer of silk that curves down perfectly to allow her sister petal to shine. A soft, lovely fragrance surrounds me and I close my eyes. In spite of the chaos, the worry and sadness in the world outside, my soul finds peace. And I remember my mother's words. Yes, Mom, you were right. So very right.

☼

Winds of Change

Like giant pinwheels they dotted the horizon throughout rural America. In the Thirties the eight-foot wheels whirled, bringing forth water when none fell from the sky. They appeared on homesteads and in pastures, allowing livestock to graze in places where no ponds existed. The tall, sturdy machines remained part of our farm heritage for another forty years.

The wonderful windmill utilized the power of the wind to pump much-needed water. The wide blades on the circle at the top caught the wind, turning a rotor, which drove a pump rod up and down. The rod forced water from the well hundreds of feet below the ground to the top of a pipe. Sure as the wind, the cycle repeated over and over until water bubbled up, overflowing into a storage tank

The towering windmill on our South Dakota farm huddled next to the fence of the cattle yard. The round storage tank was made of wood, bolted together on expansive metal bands. A board fence butted the edge of the tank on one side and a post which held a swinging metal gate on the other, giving access to half of the open tank to the cattle in their area and half to us on the opposite side near the house.

(Sherri Webb)

A five-year-old tends to take life for granted. The sight of that spinning disk and the clicking sound of the rod was the norm for me, simply a machine that produced water on demand, and in my young mind it would keep turning forever. I watched Mom, Dad or my siblings release the rough wooden lever from its holding position in the bend of one of the steel legs to "turn on" the device. I watched when they pulled the handle down, locking it in place, stopping the mill. A full tank of water welcomed the thirsty cows, sure as the Dakota wind.

One hot, muggy day the sky darkened suddenly as an ominous black cloud scudded under the sun. A storm required fast action to protect lives and property. As Dad and my siblings ran outside, Dad called, "Somebody turn off the windmill!" I headed for the tower. The lever extended from the steel support at a 45-degree angle. I was not very tall, and certainly not thin, but somehow I managed to reach the end of that wooden stick with both hands. With all my might I tried pulling it down, but the wind increased, and the wheel above spun wildly as I hung from the handle, feet dangling. Only a few seconds passed and Dad was there to pull down the bar. I was pretty sure I saw a twinkle flash in those hazel eyes before he ordered me to get to the house.

The metallic clanging of the pump rod was part of farm life, a comforting, reassuring sound, indicating that there would always be water, though someone had to remember to turn on the windmill when the cattle would come home to drink and turn it off when the tank was full. Occasionally it ran over and the cattle enjoyed a refreshing mud bath for their cloven hooves. I remember them dipping their heads into the tank and slurping in water until I thought they would surely empty the vessel. Then big brown eyes lifted to me, and with water dripping from their chins, they turned back to the pasture.

The whirling circle with a tail that rotated it to face the wind was a blur in the sunset, a pleasant amenity I knew I could count on. Yes, life was good, but I was not the one that had to climb to the top and oil the rotor. That was my older brother Don's job. He climbed to the top of that 27-foot tower with the oil can. There were footholds along one leg, like a skimpy ladder. I don't remember being warned not to climb it, nor do I remember attempting the feat. Once in a while, Dad or Delmer trekked partway up to see if cattle had escaped the pasture fence or check on something far in the distance.

A neighbor recalled how his grandmother's windmill, which stood in the barnyard, saved his hide twice when an angry mother cow considered him a threat to her newborn calf. Footwork and quick climbing delivered him to safety, just out of the reach of the cow's sharp horns and thrashing hard head.

Time passed. The wheel on that windmill turned millions of times. My memories changed to pulling down a small metal lever with a circle on the end, the pump jack. In the blink of an eye, electricity took over the work of the old steel windmill.

The sturdy tower still stands on the home place, but the whirling wheel has been removed. It is no longer needed to bring forth life-giving waters from deep in the earth. Times change.

Driving through the countryside, I still see an occasional windmill standing tall and proud on the horizon, a reminder of days long gone, and, like a cool summer breeze, the memories flow from the nooks and crannies of my mind.

Food for Thought

"You watch for the big hand to be on the twelve and the little hand to be on the four." My sister Dorothy remembers Dad explaining how she would know when to bring lunch out to the field. Barely five and the only one available that summer afternoon, she took her responsibility seriously. Sitting at the kitchen table, she stared up at the round metallic clock on the wall. The seconds ticked away, but to a young child the hands moved at a snail's pace. Finally, it was four o'clock and she grabbed the bucket and, blonde braids bouncing, she skipped up the gravel road. The girl and her farmer father sat and talked in the shade of the tractor tire while he ate his bologna sandwich and drank homemade lemonade from a quart jar. When it was time to get back on the tractor, they hid the pail in the grass next to a wooden fence post, then Dad lifted Dorothy up on the tractor. Legs tucked under the steering rod, she happily rode with him once around the field.

Our mother, directly involved in the farm operation, also took her job seriously. Lunches to the guys in the field always included dessert, usually homemade cookies stacked in a small coffee can. On cool days, our father savored hot coffee from a thermos. When we girls were the lunch bearers, we often came home with an orange Kool Aid mustache. No matter how warm the South Dakota sun, nor how far we walked, we all enjoyed lunch break.

Waiting in the grassy fence rows for the steady putt-putt sound of the approaching tractor, we inevitably found something interesting to

Dorothy with Dad.
(Dorothy Holter)

watch. If the guys were plowing, graceful white gulls flitted and swirled around the plow, scooping up earthworms from the freshly turned soil. Striped gophers chattered their alarm call as they scooted down their holes. A mound of soft black soil protruded like a small mountain beside a badger burrow.

Mom relished the time, too. Sometimes she walked with us but more often drove to the field. My brother Delmer reminisces that when it got to be mid-afternoon he started watching for the light blue pickup to drive in as he approached the end of the field on each round. With a smile, she lugged the parcels, pleased to spend time with her son. When Mom brought lunch to Dad, she listened to his update of progress and they made plans for the next day; it was a peaceful time spent together.

Many years later, my siblings and I treasure fond memories of the days of the afternoon lunch breaks, a part of farm life. Our less-active lifestyles no longer require the extra energy of a snack to sustain us until dinner, though each day at four o'clock I strangely find myself hungry for one of Mom's chocolate chip cookies! Looking back, I realize that the lunches in the field were not so much about the food. As youngsters, we witnessed and became a part of a thoughtful, caring ritual that spoke volumes. The folks knew lunch in the field provided a needed break from the round-after-round monotony for the farmer. Lessons in nature and quality time with Dad nurtured us as we grew, and we learned the value of communication, one-on-one, face-to-face, uninterrupted conversation. In today's world that is definitely food for thought.

Until the Cow Comes Home

Time to milk the cow! Six o'clock AM. Six o'clock PM. Every day. No matter what, Bessie, our gentle brown and white Guernsey, had to be milked. The milking chores were part of life on the farm, and the six growing youngsters welcomed the gallons of milk she produced. Plentiful Guernsey milk meant meals with vegetables swimming in the white richness, homemade butter and ice cream and best of all, whipped heaven that was made from the cream that Mom skimmed from the top of the milk after it set for a day. Mmmm. Strawberry shortcake topped with a huge dollop of fluffy, sweet whipped cream made June "Dairy Month" at our house long before it was even imagined.

At the early morning session (during which time I was nestled snug in my bed), Dad or Mom's skilled hands brought forth the foaming white liquid into the three-gallon metal pail. Mom was used to milking. She often reminisced of her growing-up days when she and her sisters milked thirty Holsteins by hand before and after school. At our farm our older brother Donald usually did the evening milking.

In the morning Bessie waited in the barnyard, ready for the door to open. Eager for her breakfast treat of cracked corn and oats served up in her special trough, she would hurry into the barn, push her head through the stanchions and start chewing before you could say, "Don't cry over spilt milk!" Then Dad or Mom would lock the stanchion gate, pull up the one-footed milk stool, and push his or her head into the cow's hip joint, preventing a hoof in the bucket. Soon the rhythmic "quish-quish" sound began, and the level of white rose quickly in the pail.

Evening milking required a different routine as Bessy had been released to the expansive pasture that morning. By milking time, most nights she stood chewing her cud contentedly far, far from the barn. My three sisters or their younger brother remember being responsible for bringing the cow home. Each day one or two of them climbed over the wooden barnyard fence and hastened out to the pasture. Adventure beckoned as bare feet padded on the soft dirt paths created by the cows as they strolled single-file through the grass. Fresh "cow pies" were easily avoided on the well-worn trail. A shallow crick rippled across the meadow into the neighboring field.

In one spot three rough rocks jutted above the water, providing dry passage to the other side.

My sister Dorothy recalls one day as she skipped along the cow path, she spotted a slight movement on the first stone. She stopped short. A striped snake lolled there, red tongue flitting as it coiled on the sun-warmed surface. Bessie probably heard the fearful shriek as Dorothy instantly detoured to the much longer route up the hill. She crossed in the shallow water next to the shelter belt of trees. When Bessie saw the girl approaching, she simply started plodding home, each step just a wee bit faster than the last as her full udder swayed back and forth, bouncing against her hind legs.

Being the youngest, the memories that flow from the nooks and crannies of my mind are different from my siblings. I remember a very tall step that had to be navigated to get into the first door of the barn, the one that led into the milking room. One short leg reached for the top, then the other. As I stood there, eyes adjusting to the dim light of the barn, I suddenly felt a spray of warm liquid splashing in my face! Ah! My brother Don was milking and obviously had practiced aim. Unlike the two cats who sat waiting on each side of the milk stool, happily washing their milky faces, I was not thrilled with the unexpected face-bath. As any five-year-old girl would do, I placed my hands on my hips and scolded that older brother of mine, ending my rant with, "I'm gonna tell!" He responded with a mischievous grin and another on-the-mark squirt, just before he stood and poured some of Bessie's milk into a metal pie tin for the smiling cats.

Most of our memories of growing up with a family milk cow are happy, some delicious. The daily demands of milking taught us responsibility, the need to work together and the value of having a sense of humor. Little did we know then that, thirty-five years before the dairy industry launched their "Got milk?" campaign, the milk mustache was born. Yes, it all began with a stream of Bessie's milk whizzing through the air in the big red barn on our South Dakota farm.

☼

You Just Keep Going

A drive through the country. This was not the typical leisurely Sunday drive. No, this trip was different. Early that morning, a hailstorm had ripped through the area. It began with an occasional clunk here and there on the roof. Then the pounding grew to a dreadful, deafening racket that sought to smother us as we sat in the kitchen, waiting, willing it to stop. The horrible clatter went on for more than twenty minutes.

Dad's face was solemn as we turned down the road that led to the fields. Less than a half mile and we came upon the storm's devastation. What had yesterday been a lush field of green plants with shiny long leaves reaching for the sun had become a tattered carpet from which protruded tarnished sticks, what was left of the young corn stalks. A sour smell drifted into the car's open windows as the remnants of hailstones turned to haze in the morning sun.

From the back seat I saw Mom steal a look at her husband, love and concern glistening through the wetness in her soft blue eyes. We drove on in silence to another pillaged field. Finally, I could stand the ominous stillness no longer. "Will we be all right, Dad?"

His quick glance in the rear-view mirror revealed six somber faces. A slight smile lit his face, and he answered softly, "Yeah, we will be all right." He drove on for a few moments in thought, then went on. "We'll have plenty

Harley Holter checking his field.
(Aaron Holter)

of hay for the livestock. And maybe we can still get a crop of millet from this field." Spirits lightened as we released a collective sigh of relief. The message came through, loud and clear: you just keep going.

My brother-in-law tells the story of a disastrous storm near Platte, South Dakota. He was working with his dad in the field when a huge black cloud hurtled into view. They raced for home in their '48 Chevy pickup, but the hail did not wait. The golf-ball sized ice chunks slammed into the windshield, shattering the entire surface in seconds. The man and his son held their farmer straw hats against the surface in front of them to prevent flying glass splinters from striking their faces.

Fortunately, years of total crop loss from hail were few and far between, but nearly every year the rain stopped for some period of time in eastern South Dakota during the fifties and sixties. Corn leaves turned brown far too soon as small ears emerged. Some years, drought allowed little growth on oats and it ripened barely six inches tall. I remember Dad and my brothers discussing whether or not the combine would be able to pick up the light windrows.

Our parents grew up on farms during the Great Depression and the continual drought of the thirties. Sometimes they would reminisce of the hardships endured, but they always added a positive note. "We never went hungry." "Sometimes at school, the town kids had no food to bring, but we always had something in our lunch pails." One of Mom's friends announced one day that she was going to marry a farmer. "They always have something to eat!"

Dad used to speak of the farms that were lost during that desolate time in history. "If those farmers could have just stuck it out another year or two, they would have made it," he conjectured. "There were good farming years after that."

My sisters tell of happy times amidst the devastation of nature's defiance. Sometimes, after weeks of hot weather without a drop of rain, we were allowed to run and splash when the welcome downfall finally came. Once, after a hail storm, the girls gathered the small pebbles of ice in buckets and we used them to freeze ice cream in the old crank freezer. "When life gives you hail….."

One day a battered pickup pulled into the front yard as our father was about to climb up onto the Owatonna windrower. Dad walked to the driver's window. The young man rented a farm a few miles south of us. The conversation turned to crops, and the visitor shook his head as he grumbled, "This year my corn got set back by a late frost. Then it didn't rain for a month and the wind came up and blew dirt that sliced off the plants. Then what was left got riddled with hail. Don't know if there will be a crop or not." He pounded his fist on the steering wheel and hung his head. "What do ya do?"

Dad leaned against the dusty pickup fender, just next to the window. His eyes took in our Quonset, the chicken coop, barn and windmill. He heard the gentle calls of calves romping in the nearby pasture. Finally, he looked up at the house as two chattering youngsters emerged, chore buckets in hand. Then he cleared his throat and replied, "Some years are like that. In farming. In life. You just have to keep going."

Plant. Hope.

The young farmer pressed his foot down on the shoulder of the garden fork. He pushed the tines into the soil all around the hole, creating small tunnels in the black South Dakota earth. "We need to make it easy for the roots to grow," he explained to the four-year-old girl and her little brother, who stood watching. "My dad used to throw a horseshoe in the hole when he planted apples." He smiled as he remembered. "Said it added iron to the soil."

When the earthen home was ready, his wife knelt down, placed the young tree into the hole and gently pushed the loose soil around the roots. Wash dress and apron did not protect her bare knees from pressing into the newly-thawed ground. The girl and boy dropped down next to their mother and patted the earth around the tree.

At last, the family stood back to admire their work. Six small trees, spaced far apart, protruded from the soil on the east end of the garden, sticks pointing to the sky. The little boy reached for his sister's hand and their father knelt down next to them. "You two will need to help water these trees," he said. "Hopefully, someday you'll get to eat apples from them."

They did, and they did. My sister Deloris recalls carrying buckets of water to the young saplings, especially in years when rain was scarce, but the trees and the children grew up together, and before too many years, four more apple-eaters were added to the family.

Our parents grew up on farms during the Thirties. Survival demanded that they set aside food for winter and for years of scarcity. Nothing was wasted. So, when those six apple trees began to produce, Mom cooked, baked and canned every possible apple concoction, and we kids enjoyed the bounty. The aroma of apple crisp or baked apples fresh from the oven often greeted us when we got off the school bus on fall afternoons.

The Whitney crabs, small, but sweet, became pickles and sauce and juice, stashed in the basement in clear mason jars. When the Wealthy and Winesap varieties bore fruit, there was spicy, brown apple butter and chunky applesauce. Deloris, Darlene and Dorothy peeled and sliced. Jars of canned apples for pie soon joined the others on the shelves. Almost every Saturday Mom baked pies. During the winter, she folded a jar of canned apples with sugar and spices and tucked them between crusts. Sunday dinner delight!

Sometimes in the fall, frigid temperatures threatened the apples still on the tree. My brother Delmer climbed the ladder in approaching darkness to pick the remaining apples. He handed them down to my sisters, who carried buckets inside to save the fruit from frost. Mom and I wrapped the biggest, best red striped spheres in newspaper and packed them in a box in the porch. Through March we could unwrap crisp, juicy fruit. Even when they began to shrivel, they still worked in apple cake.

Some years, late spring frost killed the fragrant blossoms, or drought stressed the tall trees and the crop was sparse. But in years of bounty, Dad would reminisce about when he and Mom and Deloris and Don had planted those six young apple trees.

Autumns and Apple Pie Sundays flew by. More than twenty years after that hopeful tree-planting day, Deloris and her husband climbed into their car after a visit "back home." Suddenly, Dad hurried out of the house, carrying a five-gallon bucket loaded with apples. He opened the door to the back seat and set it on the floor. The scent of the fresh fruit filled the vehicle. He ruffled the soft blond hair of the four-year-old girl and her little brother as they smiled up at Grandpa. Then he turned to his daughter with a twinkle in his eyes and said, "Mom doesn't want these to go to waste. Hope you can use 'em." They did.

Martin Luther once said, "Even if I knew that tomorrow the world would go to pieces, I would still plant my apple tree."

MOM'S APPLE CAKE

3 cups diced, peeled apples
1 cup sugar
Let sugar and apples set for 30 minutes to form juice.
1 ½ cups flour
1 teaspoon salt
1 teaspoon baking soda
½ teaspoon baking powder
½ cup cooking oil
1 egg
2/3 cup chopped nutmeats (walnuts)
½ cup coconut.

Sift flour, salt and soda. Mix well. Add oil, egg and apple mixture all at once and mix. Fold in nuts and coconut and bake in a 9 x 13 pan at 350 degrees for 30 minutes, or until a toothpick comes out clean.

Mix the following topping and spread on the cake immediately after removing it from the oven:

6 Tablespoons softened butter

¾ cup brown sugar

4 Tablespoons cream

1/3 cup chopped nutmeats

Place the cake back into the hot oven for five minutes.

Note from author: Enjoy warm with ice cream or real whipped cream!

Old School

In spite of today's playful exaggerations about walking distance and incline, the country school experience truly played a crucial role educating youngsters in rural America during the first half of the twentieth century.

My two older sisters and brother, dinner pails swinging from their hands, trekked one and a half miles (not ten, and not uphill both ways) to their one-room schoolhouse. The simple white structure provided a center of learning for not only the three Rs, but also music, art, science and life. Five year olds and teenagers sat in the same classroom. Different age groups took turns with the teacher at the recitation bench and absorbed bits and pieces from the other sessions as well.

The long walks to school ended for Deloris, Don and Darlene when they completed sixth, fourth and second grades, and the Rose Hill District Number 12 School closed its doors. Bus rides, separate classrooms and school lunches soon supplemented their curriculum, but the old-school lessons endured. Public school in the small town of Erwin, South Dakota, provided the new house of learning for them and later their four younger siblings.

Our memories of school are all different, and some probably should not appear in print! Incidents, emotions, tastes and smells melded school to life and encompassed far more than textbooks. Stiff new shoes felt strange on the feet after a summer of romping barefoot. Whiffs of school paste and new crayons inspired creative instincts as we walked in the large classroom door. Maps of the world and the United States, tightly wound on wooden dowels, waited to be pulled down by a string. Chalk "scritched" on the blackboard when teacher or student scribed.

Long metal tables with attached benches lined the lunchroom as students filed in, youngest first. The head cook, Minnie, always greeted us with a smile. We followed our tray as she dished up our choices from the huge kettles containing that day's menu items. Fridays meant fish sticks. We could have two or three or four. Children needed sustenance, after all! A spoon of green beans and a huge dollop of mashed potatoes soon accompanied the fish. Then Minnie ladled a generous portion of melted butter into the center well on those potatoes. The yellow pool rippled as we carefully carried our tray to the milk machine in the corner. White or chocolate perfectly accompanied the frosted peanut butter dessert bar. After dropping two pennies in the money jar, we lifted the big knob over our glass and watched the liquid stream out of the hollow white rubber tube.

Noon recess followed lunch, and after workouts on swings, merry-go-rounds, teeter totters and jungle gyms, we filed back into our classrooms. Desks were important, like home away from home. In first grade, there were different sizes, so we had to try them out for the correct fit, the Goldilocks standard. Older grades had bigger desks. Some were bolted onto boards, the cast iron feet curving up to a wooden chair. The seat was attached to the flat writing area of the person behind. Random sloppy penmanship might be blamed on the fidgety kid sitting in front of you. Well, maybe once…

In later years we sat in desks with an open front compartment for books and papers. A small hole, once intended as an ink well for fountain pens, repurposed as a receptacle for short pencils or love notes. My favorite desks were the ones with a hinged lid that covered the large sink-like compartment where we stored our menagerie of textbooks, writing tools and personal items. That lid allowed secret communication with the person across the aisle. We could lift the lid straight up and hold it there while we hunkered down behind it and silently "spoke" to our neighbor. Some of us studying

Erwin School. (Dorothy Holter)

78

Lip Reading 101 became quite proficient until the teacher noticed adjacent desk covers standing open for long periods of time. Busted!

The "library" consisted of a bookshelf in the back of the room with just enough volumes to finish them all by the end of the year. The problem was, sometimes low student numbers necessitated combining classes, and I remained in the same room for two consecutive years. By the end of the second year I had read The Long Winter enough times to hear blizzards in my sleep.

One music teacher taught all grades and accompanied the singing on the big, old, upright piano in the music room. As third graders, we proudly belted out "My Country 'Tis of Thee" every week. Sometimes we sang silly songs. On occasion, a tiny school memory pops out of the nooks and crannies of my brain like a bubble and I find myself singing (very quietly) "Kookaburra sits on the old gum tree, merry, merry king of the bush is he..."

We learned, grew up, and graduated. The crayon-paste aroma welcomed new children. Desks, books, songs and lunch menus changed. "New and updated" replaced "old" in classrooms and teaching methods. But still today, Old School Memories receive the highest grade—top-of-the-class A plus!

On the Town

It was a Saturday evening in late September around 1959. A brief thunderstorm had just passed through; sheets of rain pounded and splashed the earth. Then just as abruptly, the rain stopped.

The John Deere 520 rumbled into the driveway and headed for the Quonset, pulling the corn picker, its three pointy snouts bouncing over the gravel.

Delmer and Don had finished feeding the hogs. The open sides of their five-buckle overshoes flapped as they met Dad at the front gate. I followed them inside, wondering why our father was in such a good mood after his corn harvest had been rained out.

The men washed in the small sink at the end of the large room that served as kitchen and dining room. Darlene and Dorothy were setting the table. Mom sliced the ring bologna in the cast iron skillet, and Deloris dished the crisp-fried potatoes.

Dad's eyes twinkled as he sat at his place at the table next to Mom. "Want to go to town tonight? He rubbed his hand over his bald head and grinned. "Think I need a haircut."

Mom chuckled and her gaze flashed to her husband's shiny crown, but she hurried to get supper under way. Our mother seldom turned down a trip to town.

Dad glanced around the table at six expectant faces. "You kids want to come along? You might see somebody you know." We picked up the chewing pace. Like Mom, we enjoyed going about anywhere. "Be good for you to get out."

In twenty minutes we were ready to go. Dad reached into his pocket and pulled out a handful of change. He fished out six dimes and handed one to each of us. "You can spend it if you want. Buy some candy that'll rot your teeth out. Or you can save it and get enough to buy something that will last." I thought of the ice skates with the shiny silver blades in the Sears-Roebuck catalog.

Soon Dad was parking the car on Calumet Avenue in the small town of De Smet, South Dakota.

With the handles of her brown purse over her arm, Mom stepped toward the grocery store, list in hand.

The boys followed Dad two blocks up the street to the shop where the red diagonal stripes on the barber pole curled up and disappeared. The barber sat in his own chair. Two men lolled comfortably on black vinyl seats and greeted Dad and the boys as they settled in. The banter soon turned to the weather, farming, and the corn crop. An hour later Delmer began to fidget. Dad paid the barber two bits for his haircut, and the bell over the door clanged as someone strode in. Another farmer. Delmer sighed.

Meanwhile, as my sisters and I entered the Ben Franklin dime store, two young boys sauntered out, each clutching a small paper bag. One was unwrapping a stick of Black Jack gum. They glanced our way but did not seem very friendly. Just inside the door the candy display beckoned. Rows and shelves of bars and boxes and bags emitted an enticing aroma of cherry, mint and chocolate. I spotted the white and brown box of Milk Duds, chewy caramel drops coated with chocolate. My favorite! I squeezed the dime in my pocket. I envisioned twirling over frozen Spirit Lake in my brand-new ice skates. I hurried to catch up with my sisters.

Why were they looking at dish towels? My sister Deloris filed through the embroidery iron-ons. "Christmas will be here before we know it, and I want to get ideas for presents." Darlene and Dorothy thought Mom would like the days of the week pattern. My hand still clutching the coin, I sighed and decided the skates could wait until next year.

Mom and the kids. Dorothy, Deloris, Darlene, Don, Delmer, DeAnn, Mom.

After browsing every aisle, the four of us hurried outside to continue our night on the town. A television blared from the background as a girl stepped out of the furniture store. The classmate exchanged pleasantries with Dorothy for a few minutes and went on her way. Darlene reached for my hand as we crossed Calumet to the other side. Lights flashed from the theater entry. Even with the double doors closed, the smell of fresh, buttery popcorn drifted out as we strolled by. My tummy grumbled. The sisters decided we had better head back to the car in case the others were waiting.

Mom smiled as we piled in and waited with her. Fifteen minutes later Delmer and Don showed up. "Where's Dad?" I asked. Delmer rolled his eyes. "He's talkin' to somebody, AGAIN."

Dad finally appeared on the sidewalk. His eyes searched the car, taking a mental roll call of the family. Just then a neighbor strolled out of the grocery store in front of him and the men shook hands. Delmer groaned. "Oh, no! C'mon, Dad!" Visions of Milk Duds danced in my head.

At last, Dad opened the car door. "Did you buy ice cream?" he asked Mom.

"I didn't know how long you would be." (Loving-wife subtlety.)

Dad headed into the grocery store and returned, a paper bag under his arm. Soon we were back around the kitchen table, mouths watering as Mom scooped the creamy pink goodness into bowls--strawberry ice cream!

As we savored and swirled the bits of strawberries over our tongues, Dad looked around the table at his four daughters and two sons. He beamed, then asked innocently, "Did you enjoy your night in town? It's good for you to get out once in a while." We kept our eyes on our ice cream.

Surprise Inside

Elbows on the counter, I watched as Mom carefully pried the top corner from the blue and red box. The words on the front foil wrap boldly proclaimed "Free Glass Inside!" A giant starburst twinkled brightly on the picture of the tall glass tumbler. "Duz does everything!" was printed at the bottom of the carton. Guess it did, as my mother beamed as she pulled out the smoky-blue treasure. She rinsed and dried it until it sparkled like the picture and fondly placed it next to the other three on the top cupboard shelf.

There is an element of excitement about getting something free, and manufacturers used the sales tactic to their advantage, especially following the bleak years of the World Wars and the Great Depression. After long periods of doing without so there would be enough for the soldiers or struggling to feed the family, it must have been fun to get something pretty—especially when it came free!

Duz did it again when they included a 22K Golden Wheat dish in every box. Monday washings enabled American housewives to collect plates, cups, and saucers nice enough to grace the table when company visited. Even cooked oatmeal was special when served in "crystal" bowls that came free in Crystal Wedding Oats canisters.

A Cannon bath towel snuggled in every package of Breeze laundry soap. The clothes on the line fairly gleamed with the brightness from all the detergent purchased!

Companies quickly discovered who made the food-buying decisions in the family—the children! Cracker Jack plopped a prize in every box, beginning in 1912. For more than a century, kids couldn't wait to open the small bonus, a metal or plastic toy or a baseball card.

Kellogg was the first manufacturer to offer prizes in their cereal, and others soon followed suit. "Snap," "Crackle," and "Pop" figurines stood by as we listened while pouring milk over the crispy morsels of rice. Wheaties boxes boasted of the "real" microscope inside, a plastic device that magnified things six times. Attached to the box of one cereal was an actual 45 record. It didn't matter that we had never heard of the band or the song. It played!

Hidden in boxes of Wheat and Rice Honeys was a free 2 Stage Rocket that separated in mid-air when launched. In 1958 Nabisco Spoonmen,

"Munchy," "Crunchy," and "Spoon-size," (They ran out of "unchies"?) attached to a child's spoon, assisting as he or she scooped up little squares of the shredded grain.

During the sixties, youngsters could complete their espionage repertoire by buying all three kinds of Chex: rice, corn and wheat. With a Secret Agent ring, watch, and decoder pencil in hand, we had it all. We could practice our spy technique while watching our atomic submarine (Wheaties freebie) crash-dive and resurface with Frogmen (Kellogg's Cornflakes) swimming along beside.

One afternoon, as I was strolling through the grocery aisles with my mother, I spotted the endcap display of neatly stacked Kellogg's boxes with the vivid sign above: "Free Dragnet Whistle inside every box!" Immediately, the theme song of my favorite TV show trumpeted in my head: DUM da dum-dum. I heard the solemn announcer: "The story you are about to see is true. The names have been changed to protect the innocent." I envisioned my hero, Sgt. Joe Friday. I NEEDED that whistle. "Mom, can we please buy cornflakes?"

I stared wistfully at the picture of the whistle on the box as I put it away in the cabinet at home. Mom insisted that we finish all the "old" stuff before we could open new. Waiting for that prize was like anticipating Christmas in September. I thought it would never come.

I had to be patient. Joe Friday was patient. At night I dreamed of chasing down the bad guys. I blew my whistle and they stopped and held up their hands. I hauled them in to the precinct.

The dilemma was real the morning I could finally open the box. Of course, the prize was hiding at the bottom. A choice had to be made. Dig in with both hands and fish it out? Eat the whole box? Wait a few days and risk that a brother or sister might find it first?

Mother's big enamel bowl held most of the flakes; the distinct aroma of corn drifted up as I emptied the box. Finally, out dropped the coveted red whistle, wrapped in crinkly, clear cellophane. Flakes flew as I grabbed it. With a delighted grin, I slipped it into my pocket.

One cup at a time I began pouring that cereal back into the crisp white package. The fine print at the bottom of the ingredients list, "contents may settle during shipment," was an understatement. At last the huge bowl was empty and the paper package stuffed back into the box. My breakfast bowl overflowed only slightly with the flakes that wouldn't fit. I poured in milk, lifted a spoonful and chewed away as I examined the carton in front of me.

Wait! What was that? What was printed on the white circle on the bottom front corner? "Coming soon! A powerful Superman Belt and Buckle in specially marked boxes. Help Superman save the world. Don't miss it!"

I stared at the bulging box before me. I poured myself another bowl.

☀

Head 'em Up! Move em Out!

"Rollin', rollin', rollin'...." Frankie Laine's smooth voice drifted into the kitchen, signaling the beginning of our favorite western. My brother penciled one more division problem, then closed the text with a final thump. I hurriedly ran the towel over the cast iron kettle and carried it to the cupboard. No television allowed until homework and chores were done.

Delmer and I knew the lyrics by heart and just how much time we had before the opening monologue. "Cut 'em out, ride 'em in." A distinctive whip crack followed each "HiAH." At the very end, two cracks resounded just before the final shout: "RAWHIDE!"

Just in time we scrambled to the living room rug in front of the television. Trail boss Gil Favor (Eric Fleming) introduced the episode. The drovers moved thousands of cattle from San Antonio, Texas, to Sedalia, Missouri. Danger lurked on the trail. Parched plains, anthrax, wolves, and bandits threatened. Gil and his crew, particularly his trusty ramrod, Rowdy Yates (Clint Eastwood, who had not yet reached stardom), braved the perils of the 700-mile drive. On cue, the herd started off as Gil gave the command: "Head 'em up! Move 'em out!" (whip crack).

So, two weeks later we reckoned we were ready for our own trail drive. In early summer, the family moved our herd of less than 100 cattle about a mile down the road to the south pasture. There they grazed contentedly on tall grasses and drank from the stock dam. Before winter we brought them back to the pastures close to home where the new calves would be born.

Moving cattle involved many drovers, and we all dreaded the event. Without fail, a cow would decide to sample greener grass, or a calf would kick into teenage rebellion mode and gallop off into the sunset. We sensed Dad's tension as he instructed his crew. He and Don would bring the herd from the yard at home with the tractor and get them started. Mom, Dorothy and Darlene were to take the pickup and cover the intersection a half mile up the trail. Mom and the pickup would park on one side, and the two girls would be ready on the west. Hopefully, no vehicles would approach while the critters were crossing. Deloris was stationed at the neighbor's driveway. Delmer and I guarded the approach to the oat field. The lush green carpet shimmered in the evening sun as the South Dakota breeze brushed over it. "Don't let them get in the oats. We don't need that trampled," our father instructed sternly as we took our positions just inside the opening to the field.

I nervously adjusted my cowgirl hat, black straw with a white band on the brim. It was not crooked and battered like Rowdy's, but it had a string tie that hung under my chin, just like his. Delmer assumed trail boss role. "It'll be all right, Sis. Once the lead cow goes by, all the others will follow. We just make sure she stays on the road."

I thought, "Sure, Gil," and headed for the fence line to find a stick. We couldn't see any cattle coming yet, so we both found dead branches, the sight of which would strike fear in the most wayward bovine. We were ready!

Soon we heard mothers call to their young as they turned from the driveway and headed our way. Heads bobbed as the leaders jogged up the road. Delmer motioned me to come closer to their path. We held our breaths, sticks ready, as the lead cow and her followers hurried by, up the road toward Deloris. With a sigh of relief, my brother turned to me and his silver braces flashed brightly. "We did it!" Hooves crunched on gravel as cows and calves passed. Gil and Rowdy would have been downright proud.

Our thrill of victory was cut short suddenly by a wide gap in the herd. Confused calves bawled for their mothers and turned back to the driveway. In the middle of the road, just short of our post, the two Charolais bulls were fighting! They butted heads, twisted, and turned. We watched in horror as their battle brought them closer and closer to us. They swerved off the road into the grass, directly into our oat field. Clumps of dirt flew around them. We yelled "HiAH,"and waved the sticks frantically. One bull went down on his knees. Delmer grasped the opportunity and crashed the weapon down hard on its rump. It cracked on impact, and my brother stepped back as shaggy-crested heads lunged, unfazed.

Frozen in place, I stared helplessly. My trail boss brother grabbed my hand and we scooted up to the fence line, far from the flying feet.

The last of the herd passed on the road while we watched the fight. Finally, our unhappy father maneuvered the John Deere 520 around the crazed creatures, into the oats. The feud for male dominance subsided, and the tractor followed the scrappers as they trotted to catch their throng.

Delmer tossed the remainder of the stick to the ground and we walked home dejectedly. We did the best we could with what we had, but the bulls had still trampled the oats. We wondered what Gil and Rowdy would have done.

The whip. That's it! Maybe the formidable sound of that whip cracking would have turned those crazed bulls back to the road.

This fall. Next cattle drive we would be ready!

Apple Butter Therapy

Nothing is more memorable than a smell. Scent, memories and emotions are closely intertwined and today, the aroma of a home is big business. Candles, diffusers, spritzers and soaps of various essences can elicit distinct emotional responses. One can be energized, calmed, relieved of stress or filled with a sense of well-being and happiness simply by breathing.

As is the case with most modern-day sciences, our mothers and grandmothers were practicing aromatherapy long before it came in vogue. The annual apple butter day in our South Dakota farmhouse kitchen was such an event. The aroma and emotions of the day emanate from the nooks and crannies of my mind; it was the ultimate "comfort" experience.

The apple butter tradition required many hands and everyone in the family pitched in. On a cool, crisp October morning Delmer and I headed to the orchard to fill buckets with windfalls, bird-sampled, and small apples that remained. None could be wasted, and apple butter was the perfect ending for them.

Darlene and Dorothy rinsed and sorted the apples in the kitchen sink, trimming off blemishes and quartering the larger ones. Mom added water and soon four kettles simmered on the cook stove over her perfect combination fuel of corncobs and wood chunks. The kitchen warmed quickly, and soon the lovely fragrance of cooking apples permeated the room. Mom brought out the huge blue graniteware kettle from the porch, and we arranged all the needed supplies.

Once the apples were cooked, Deloris and Mom ladled small amounts into the Foley food mill. The older girls took turns cranking the red wooden handle that turned a curved blade which forced the chunky substance through the mill. A tan apple sauce filled the bowl below the Foley. The peels, cores and stems that remained in the machine were emptied, batch by batch into the chicken treat bucket. Even the "girls" enjoyed apple butter therapy!

Mom emptied each full bowl of apple butter makings into the huge blue kettle on the stove, and added sugar, cinnamon and salt. Then she went about preparing the second olfactory segment of the classic event while the rest of us took turns stirring the contents in the huge vessel.

Over the next several hours we scraped the bottom of the kettle with the long wooden spoon every few minutes. Too long between stirs and the thick solution at the bottom would scorch. The amazing aura of the cinnamon-apple blend would not allow us to forget, and we happily persevered with the task. As we mixed, bubbles rose to the top and burst, sending the pleasant aroma up to our noses. Tummies growled. The butter thickened as the day wore on. We kept stirring.

Dad and Don checked in and took turns at the kettle, then headed back outside, anticipating the taste test to come. Chores awaited, but a few of us remained behind to keep up the wooden spoon brigade.

After a while, the brown apple sweetness thickened to spreading consistency and the three older girls helped our mother ladle it into pint jars, place a lid on top and twist a metal ring down tightly. Caps gave a satisfying "pop" as the jars cooled and sealed. Sixteen pints gleamed on the counter, evidence of the day's work, but we made sure plenty of apple butter remained in the kettle for later.

Meanwhile, another enticing fragrance wafted from the oven and filled our senses. It added to and intensified the apple butter aroma. Another unforgettable emotion-evoking smell.

In short order, chores were done and supper was on the table, but the very first thing we put on our plates that night was a fresh slice of homemade bread, slathered with creamy butter and spread thick to the very edges with a coating of warm, spicy-sweet apple butter. The taste and smell of comfort, happiness and love, all combined to make wonderful memories.

Possibly, present-day big business should come up with a new aromatherapy scent for their candles and diffusers, one that will evoke very pleasant emotions: Warm Apple Butter. But, if they give us Warm Apple Butter, we are probably going to want Fresh Homemade Bread to go with it.

Out on a Limb

I have chickens. My chickens are spoiled. Family and friends enjoy sharing social media posts about the latest fun fads available for my feathered friends. Always, there is a smiley emoji attached, along with the words, "Your chickens need this!" Contented brown hens lounge in comfort and style, adorned in lacy aprons or fuzzy jackets. The latest device designed to ban bird boredom—a chicken swing. Hens happily swaying back and forth, relaxing with the motion. Hmmm. Birds swaying on branches conjures less pleasant images from the Nooks and Crannies of my brain.

When I was eight, it was my responsibility to "close for the chickens" on our family farm. Weather permitting, the girls spent the day outside happily ranging for bugs and greens in the South Dakota sunshine. Before darkness they returned (hopefully) to their coop. To keep them safe from predators, the doors needed to be shut during the night. Around dusk I headed first to the hen house where all the wise-to-the world women rested on the roosts, already crooning their sleep songs. I pulled the screen door shut and hooked it securely.

In summer and fall I had one more chore to complete. Another flock of chickens resided fifty yards south of the hens in the brooder house. These were the pullets that had grown from peeping balls of fluff to potential egg factories. The younger girls also roamed outside each day in their area between the hog and cattle pastures. Like the older hens, the pullets were supposed to go inside at night to warmth and safety.

As with most teenage crowds, there has to be a few who push the limits. Maybe they were "feeling their oats." Maybe they just wanted to sleep under the stars. Possibly the birds enjoyed swaying back and forth in the gentle breezes. Whatever the reasons, unfailingly, three to five feathered fowl perched outside on the lower branches of the two ash trees growing next to the coop. Somehow, the curfew crashers needed to get inside with their sisters. But, how?

Reasoning mixed with a bit of drama. I yelled. "Raccoons are gonna get you! Cougars and foxes will eat you up!" Five white bodies ignored me.

I could just reach one of the branches. I grabbed it and shook it as hard as I could. Two pullets cackled and flew to the ground. I watched as they scrambled to the small front door of the brooder. Three remained, staring down at me, defiantly. Searching the ground, I discovered several small, partly-rotted boards. It took a few throws, but eventually, I hit close enough to scare the final three out of hiding.

For a few weeks, I managed to get all the critters in without much trouble. Then I noticed they were flying farther up into the trees, out of reach. Even the crashing boards did not faze them. Another search of the area revealed a long dead branch. (I wondered if my older siblings had used the same methods.) With a bit of maneuvering, I managed to poke the branch through the tree, close enough to achieve the desired result, everyone grounded and safe inside.

One night it was pitch-dark when I hurried out to close for the chickens. Flashlight in hand, I dared to hope that possibly all had gone in without my gentle persuasion. Well, life can never be easy, and chicken peer pressure is strong I discovered, shining the light through the trees. As if knowing I would be late, the young rebels had convinced four more little sneaks to join the slumber party. And they sat on the highest branch!

A combination of shaking, yelling and poking brought down all of those biddies except one. That feathered fiend just hunkered down closer to her ash tree roost! Beady chicken eyes glared down at me, daring me to dethrone her. Visions of drumsticks danced in my head, and not the kind in the percussion section. Chicken nuggets suddenly gained new appeal.

I won't say I was scared of the dark, but I did have a very vivid imagination. Thoughts of cougars and foxes and raccoons scared me more than the chickens. My heart pounded. Adrenaline sometimes has its advantages. I grabbed a piece of board, reared back and hurled it as hard as I could up into the depths of that tree. Surprised squawking erupted, followed by Attila the Hunkerer wildly flailing through the air. Her landing gear obviously malfunctioned, and she skidded into the dirt, halting rather abruptly. Stunned, the cantankerous creature laid there a few seconds.

As I approached, the chicken clambered to her feet and hurtled off into the darkness. She ran in the opposite direction of the brooder house!

I don't know how long it took me to get her in that night. I chased the varmint around the granary and back under the trees. Finally, I beamed the flashlight on the coop door and waited, praying. With a soft cackle that disturbingly resembled a chicken sneer, the pullet sauntered inside.

Surprisingly, some fifty years later, I have chickens. They get treats of mealworms and rice crispies. They never become drumsticks or chicken nuggets. But, will I indulge them with the latest fad? Do my chickens need to experience the joy of swaying back and forth on a chicken swing, relaxing with the movement of the gentle breezes?

Probably not.

A Bird in the Hand

Have you ever considered how when we were children we couldn't wait to grow up and do all the things grownups do, but later, when our lives are full of responsibilities, we long for the days when we were young and had no worries?

The youngest of six growing up on our South Dakota farm, I often felt like my siblings always got to do the fun stuff, and I was stuck with the menial tasks. Of course, as I got older my help was needed, but my idea of helping differed drastically from those older and wiser, especially my brother.

In late October every year, the young pullets that had grown from "chick-hood" in the brooder house needed to be moved to the henhouse, taking over the job of egg production. The old hens who had resided there for a year or two were gone. Some were sold to neighbors. Some had been pro-cessed in Mom's magical pressure canner and would be served as creamed chicken over mashed potatoes on a cold winter night.

Moving day arrived and, enviously, I watched Delmer load five straw bales onto the hay rack hitched behind the John Deere 520 and then deftly maneuver the tractor right next to the henhouse. He tossed the bales inside and motioned to me with his too-big leather glove to come and help. I watched him push his knee into a bale as he pulled the wire ties. The wires slipped off and the yellow straw was left on the floor in a loose curve. It looked easy to me, so I tried the knee trick. Note, I say "tried." "I'll get it," my brother said. "You can spread the straw around." Resentfully, I tossed and kicked the dusty bedding through the building. Soon a fluffy, dry layer covered the coop floor and the bottoms of the nesting boxes. The henhouse was ready.

Just before dark that night, Mom, Dad, Delmer and I headed to the brooder house for the relocation operation. Dad caught six pullets from the roosts, held them by the feet, and began the walk up the hill to the henhouse. Squawking faded into the distance as Mom and Delmer each grabbed four birds. I stepped in, eager to catch one. "Sis, you just open the door for us," my older brother ordered. I looked at Mom, hoping she would see my side. She said it was important that no chickens got out, trying to make me feel better. So, I did doorman duty, all the time thinking I could not wait to grow up.

At last there were only six feathered critters waiting on the roosts. Dad caught them and was about to stride out the door. I saw my chance. "Dad, can I help carry them?" His eyes glistened with that wistful, "they have to learn sometime" parent look. He handed me one. I held it by the feet upside-down, much to the dismay of the chicken. "Can I carry two?"

I followed Dad to the henhouse with a complaining bird in each hand. As I neared the old coop, I spotted my brother. His moving job finished, Delmer hopped on the John Deere and smoothly angled it toward the Quonset. I flashed him a proud grin and tried to lift my arms higher, hoping he noticed what I was carrying. He sent me a careless glance, pushed the accelerator lever forward and hot-rodded it into the building. Showoff!

Just then the chicken in my left hand gave a loud squawk, jerked her head up, and flapped her wings. Before you could say, "chicken soup with rice" the feathered fowl was on the ground, cackling joyfully at her sudden freedom. I tried to grab her with my free hand, but she fluttered out of reach. With tears in my eyes, I carried the remaining bird to the henhouse.

We all hurried back, hoping to catch her, but she escaped under the wooden barnyard fence and disappeared in the moonlit shadows.

I got out my piggy bank after supper and counted out money to pay Mom for the chicken. "Just wait," she said. I could not sleep that night. In my imagination every coyote, raccoon, and badger in the state, plus a few African jungle predators prowled in the darkness of our yard.

The next morning I hurried outside before breakfast, praying I would find her alive. A flash of white scooted under the windmill! The escapee happily roamed through the yard, searching for food in the brown grasses. Later that evening, relief washed over me as I watched her stroll up the small ramp to the brooder house.

In spite of my failure with this growing-up adventure, the story had a happy ending, and, of course, the important thing in life is what we learn from our failures.

After supper a few nights later, I started to help Mom carry the dishes to the sink. Delmer excused himself and headed to his room. Dad lingered at the table, enjoying his coffee. I saw my chance. I drew in a deep breath and turned to my father. "Dad, when can I learn to drive the tractor?"

☼

If Buttons Could Talk

"See if you can find five more of these." Mom pressed a light brown button into my small palm, then resumed her stitching. The plastic circle was indented in the center and had four holes. A smooth ridge framed the edge.

Sitting on the floor at the foot of my mother's easy chair, knees bent and ankles crossed, I leaned over the old Folger's Coffee can in front of me, the button can. I was very familiar with the can. An image of a huge sailing ship gleamed on the front. Usually I added buttons to the collection, cutting them off old pajamas, dresses and shirts. My sisters and I often helped remove buttons, zippers and metal clasps from worn-out clothing. The threadbare parts went into the rag drawer, but Mom saved any usable fabric to sew into strips and weave into rag rugs. Nothing was wasted on our farm when I was growing up.

The two-pound can was nearly full, so I pushed my small fingers into the colorful mix and stirred them around. It wasn't long until I found one perfect match. All at once something shiny caught my eye and I grasped a pink flower shape with a sparkling center. "Is this a diamond?" my five-year-old imagination questioned.

Mom chuckled as she glanced over. "No, that came from one of Deloris' dresses when she was little. Darlene and Dorothy wore the dress, too.

I spotted a shiny brass button. There was no hole in it, but a metal wire circle protruded from the back. Before I could ask, Mom spoke. "I sewed those on Don and Delmer's overall straps. The straps held up, but I patched the knees a lot."

My Grandma Anderson as a girl.

I wasn't having any luck finding more shirt buttons, so I grabbed Dad's newspaper, spread it out and tipped the can, allowing the buttons to flow in a smooth cascade. The rainbow of colors blended into a soft blur, and the mass fell into a mound as each small shape

glided down, then nestled in next to its neighbor. The button waterfall made a soft, pleasant sound. It was almost like a whisper.

On the very top of the mound, I spotted a heart-shape that was covered in lace. I ran my fingers over the yellowed mesh and looked up at my mother. She frowned slightly. "Hmm, that is an old one."

"Was it from your wedding dress?" I asked.

She smiled wistfully. "Wedding dresses were not always white and lacy back then. There was no money for that." She must have sensed my disappointment, so she added, "No sense spending money on something we would only wear once." Mom stitched away in silence while I kept sifting. I looked up to see her blue eyes shining as she spoke again. "Ida's wedding dress was beautiful. It was light blue. Taffeta." I liked thinking of my Aunt Ida in her shiny blue wedding dress.

Suddenly, the lamplight reflected off something golden that also appeared magically at the top of the mound. It was green glass with gold specks painted on one side. I held it up for Mother to see. She thought for a moment. "I think that was on a bonnet that Julia wore when she was a little girl."

"Why would we have buttons from Aunt Julia's things in our button can?" I asked.

Mom explained that when she got married and started a family of her own, her mother gathered a bunch of buttons for Mom to take home. When she needed to replace a button that had been lost from a shirt or dress, she could usually find one. I wondered if Grandma had also gotten buttons from her mother long, long ago.

Memories flowed from the nooks and crannies of my mother's mind, and

My Aunt Julia.

while I searched for brown shirt buttons I learned about my grandmother. She was born in a sod shanty to Swedish immigrants, some of the first settlers in the area. Other babies came, but as was common in those days, some died shortly after birth. There were no hospitals and few doctors close by. Life was hard, a matter of basic survival for settlers on the South Dakota prairie.

My imagination whirled as I scanned the buttons. There were tiny battered circles, faded with age. Had my great-grandmother lovingly sewn these on a soft garment for a child that she held for only hours before the precious little life faded away? Did a small boy sport the rough metal fasteners on his overall straps before he grew up and went to war? Did my grandmother undo the tiny mother-of-pearl circles on the back of her doll's dress as she dreamed of growing up and being a mommy?

A familiar brown shape appeared and imaginings switched to reality. Soon six brown buttons lined the arm on Mom's chair. I scooped the remaining buttons back into the can and returned it to the cupboard.

Today, some sixty years later, I gaze down into the can in front of me, my button can that began back when I got married, and Mom sent a batch of buttons home with me. The colors and shapes of plastic, glass and metal beckon, and I swirl my fingers through them as I remember. I scoop a bunch into my hand, lift them and then let them cascade slowly back into the can. They shimmer and sidle back into place. As they dance gently and nestle in, I hear a soft, pleasant sound---almost like a whisper.

☼

More Tricks than Treats

Halloween is a big deal for many Americans. Consumers spend billions of dollars on decorations, costumes and candy. Today, pumpkin patches and haunted houses offer treats and entertainment for all ages and tastes, but years ago the holiday was celebrated much differently.

At school we had a Halloween "party" that consisted of treats and games the last period of the day. A couple moms brought homemade cupcakes. There were no costumes. The teacher knew some of the families did not have the time or money for such frivolities.

I remember some of my friends excitedly planning their night of Trick-or-Treating and raving about the tons of candy they would rake in. It sounded like fun, so I asked Dad that night if we could dress up and visit a few neighbors. His rather stern answer rang loud and clear; no kid of theirs was going to go out begging for candy. And we most certainly would not do any tricking! That was one of the few times I envied my town friends. The envy faded quickly when Mom got out the giant graniteware kettle and stirred up a batch of popcorn balls, the caramel kind. She said we should have something on hand in case anyone came trick-or-treating. No one ever did.

Back before Hallmark and Brach's got into the act, the day (or rather, the night) was more about tricks than treats. A post-Halloween drive to town often revealed trees swathed in draping white strips. I wonder how many tries it took to throw rolls of toilet paper into the tree tops and leave the gauzy garland draping from the branches. Considering the potential shortage of the precious commodity earlier this year, it is not likely that prank will be revived any time soon.

In the thirties, Halloween meant tricks only, and acts of vandalism were mostly limited to that night. Jokes and hilarity at the time centered on one particular prank. It happened that our father had his own story to tell about it, but he did not share it with us until years later, when we were too old for tricking. Probably he didn't want to give us any ideas!

Dad and Mom had just started out on their small farm in eastern South Dakota. No one had indoor plumbing in those days. Everyone had an outhouse, the polite word for the building in which people did their "business."

The five-foot wide, seven-foot-tall building resting over a deep hole was simply a part of life, a very necessary part.

One of the favorite pastimes of local teenagers on Halloween night was tipping outhouses. Dad knew all about toilet tipping, so when he heard noises out in the back yard he flew out the front door in a flash, shotgun in hand. Just as he rounded the corner of the house, he heard the tell-tale thud as the privy toppled to the ground. Raucous laughter followed. Dad aimed at the sky and pulled the trigger. The amusement silenced abruptly and was quickly replaced by the sound of pounding feet. Soon wild thrashing noises resounded from the underbrush that led to the road.

The next morning our outraged father strode out to survey the damage. The small building was tipped forward on its front door. The flashback of the previous night made his blood boil, wishing he had caught the culprits. About to go find Mom to help set it back up, he noticed something unusual lying on the ground, not ten feet behind the gaping hole. A billfold!

After finishing morning chores, Dad took a drive a few miles up the road to a place just outside of town. During a brief visit with the owner of the billfold and his father, our dad strongly suggested that when the young man came to get his wallet, he set the outhouse back in place.

Less than an hour later a Chevy sedan rolled into the driveway. Two young men stepped out sheepishly and followed Dad to the back yard. As they approached the fallen building, the accomplice backed away, spluttering something about being innocent. At once he noticed his friend's fist clench. The open pit stood waiting, dangerously close. A sudden gust swept over the hole and slammed into his face. The plea of innocence was gone with the wind, but a distinct odor lingered in the air. Five minutes later the outhouse was back in place, ready for use.

Never again was a toilet tipped on our farm, partly because the old privy was replaced by a brand-new cement-based structure built by Roosevelt's WPA.

Not many outhouses remain in the countryside today, but the legends live on in the nooks and crannies of our minds. As I remember our father's story, I cannot help but wonder if that toilet-tipping trick from long, long ago might have affected our family holiday.

Halloween was not a big deal at our house. Maybe we can blame the kid with the billfold.

☼

The Genuine Original All-Purpose Farm "Wagon"

"Do what you can, with what you have, where you are." Theodore Roosevelt appealed to Americans to "make do" with what they had at the time. Throughout our country's history people have met the challenge, none more admirably than the farmer. And, the machine that takes first prize for usefulness? The one and only genuine original spreader!

Also called a muck spreader, honey wagon, and a few other names that cannot be printed in this column, the manure spreader's purpose was to cast the natural fertilizer produced by farm animals onto fields to enrich the soil. Our machine was green with wooden sides and bottom, one of the first models made to be pulled by a tractor rather than a team of horses. Two conveyor chains ran along the bottom of the wagon toward the rear where an auger and beaters were attached. Levers that turned the chain movement on and off extended to the arm's reach of the tractor driver. The moving mechanisms were powered by the two wheels on the spreader. The wheels turned, moving the chain, pushing the contents through the beaters and throwing the organic matter up in the air and out the back and sides.

On our farm the implement proved practical for many tasks and was often used to carry other materials. Amazingly, every spring rocks pushed their way out of the South Dakota dirt, and farming rocks is not a practical practice, so my brother and I "picked rock." Delmer hooked the manure spreader onto the John Deere 520, and we rode out to the field, parking next to the biggest boulders. The wagon was not very high, so we hefted the heavy hunks into the wagon and hauled them to the rock pile at the end of the field.

Hay rack not handy? No problem. Use the manure spreader! Delmer and Don could pack in 15 or 20 square hay bales if they leaned a few back over the beaters. The cattle in the barnyard welcomed the sweet-smelling feed.

The wondrous wagon also proved perfect for fence repair days. The guys loaded up posts, diggers, rolls of wire and staples and maneuvered in right next to the fence in need of fixing. The tractor and spreader combination comprised the ATV of the twentieth century.

Dad and Mom told stories of an extremely unconventional use of the manure spreader, the wedding chivaree. The chivaree was an old tradition of harassing the newly-married couple as much as possible on their wedding day. Long ago, someone got the brilliant idea of stealing the bride and hauling her around town in the manure spreader, and it stuck. The bride endured the ride until the bandits returned the relieved groom's honey to him. This was obviously the origin of the alias, "honey wagon." (Now we know the rest of the story.)

In those days, most farms had livestock, and when you have livestock, manure happens. Our green refuse-hauling machine often fulfilled its intended purpose, spreading the nitrogen-rich compost onto bare fields. However, emptying the old wagon was the easy part. Filling it was a sweaty, smelly job. The men in our family usually hefted the heavy forks and shovels of straw-laden waste and tossed them into the spreader, which was parked just outside the chicken coop or hog house doors. The pungent aroma of the ammonia-rich matter compelled the guys to tug the red bandanas out of their back pockets and tie them over their nose and mouth. The red fabric was seldom used for anything other than a handkerchief. Only in dire circumstances (shoveling out a dusty grain bin, dragging a field on a windy day or an occasional bank robbery) was the red fabric used for a face mask. Forking feces was serious business!

Once the spreader was full, the tractor towed it to the waiting field where it did its duty. The tractor driver reached back and engaged the levers that moved the cargo and the beaters that shot it up and out of the wagon. This distribution of compost demonstrated the most valuable and practical use of the manure spreader, the education of the young man driving the tractor.

Meteorology, physics and driver education combined into an unforgettable lesson. Remember there were no tractor cabs then. The tractor driver was exposed to the elements, whatever elements that were thrown at him at the time. The spreader was wheel-driven. The faster the wheels turned, the farther, faster and higher the dung flew. Quite quickly, the farmer learned that wind direction, or rather driving direction, was critical. (This is also why farmers wore caps.)

When I grew up there were no signs flashing as you drove under bridges on the interstate: "Watch your speed," or "Speed kills," or "Drive, don't fly." They weren't needed. What better way to educate a teenage driver than a wheel-driven manure spreader? Driving too fast? A shower of sludge rained down his neck. Cut a quick corner? Fast-flying fertilizer might become face paint. The all-purpose manure spreader, along with its other practical uses, effectively taught safe driving techniques.

President Roosevelt would have stood behind our farming practices. He would have stood behind our creative uses of the wonderful sludge-slinging machine, but I am quite certain that the wise man never, ever stood behind a manure spreader.

And that's no compost!

Dashing Through the Snow

Once. Maybe twice a year. That was normally the number of times the Hallelujah Chorus echoed through our house following our mother's announcement, "No school today!" She would have heard it on KWAT, Watertown, the designated radio station for local weather-related cancellations.

A Snow Day did not happen very often back then in rural South Dakota. It was difficult to get the word out, and someone was bound to show up at the schoolhouse. Some people in our parents' generation were needed to help on the farm; they were not allowed to finish school, so their children's education was top priority. Regardless of the reasons, when we were kids neither snow, nor rain, nor heat kept us from our appointed duty, getting to school.

In the early years, Deloris, Donald and Darlene trekked a mile and a half to Rose Hill District #12 Country School. In good weather they walked, but wild winter winds and sizable snow drifts made travel difficult for little legs. From the nooks and crannies of their minds, my sisters Darlene and Deloris recall cozy commutes in an unconventional cart. Dad removed the wheels from a wooden grain trailer and hitched Bud and Riley to the front. An old tarp over the top kept out wind and snow. Mom heated rocks in the cook stove and wrapped them and her three school-aged youngsters in blankets and rugs for the ride. Though the drive was a bit frosty for the horses and driver, the children thought it was great fun.

A few years later buses transported the six of us to public school at Erwin. Blizzards blocked gravel roads, but county snow plows opened the main highways. Dorothy remembers riding on the flat bed in a hay bale shelter. With his John Deere 730, Dad maneuvered the hay rack over the snowy gravel roads to the main highway a mile and a half north. There we waited until bus driver Clarence pulled over and cranked open the folding door for us.

It is said that necessity is the mother of invention, and farmers are good inventors. Our farm pickup had only two-wheel drive. So, when we needed to get to school and the roads were packed with snow and ice, Don and Delmer helped Dad put chains on the tires and load a dozen hay bales in the back for weight. With the added accessories, the old pickup plowed through snowy roads like a team of huskies at the Iditarod.

No innovation could beat the blizzards of '68. I was the only one left at home and had just begun my freshman year at De Smet. Heavy snows came early, much like in The Long Winter. Even the main highways shrunk to narrow cuts with six-foot snow walls looming on both sides. At night 20 mph winds drifted them shut, making the roads impassable almost daily. Schools struggled to remain open.

Finally, the school board came up with a plan: bring the students to town. Some of us stayed with relatives, but many De Smet residents graciously opened their homes to families from the outlying area, including Bancroft. For several wintery months we became town kids. I remember thinking, "This is the life!" No chores, and I could walk to a friend's house in five minutes. Soon the novelty wore off, however, and I could not wait for the weekends when the weather allowed me to go home to the farm.

Yes, life was different when you lived in the country, especially on Snow Days. Delmer recalls those mornings and how excited some of us were. A fun day at home. No classes, no books, no school. After enjoying Mom's hearty breakfast, he bundled into warm coveralls, coat, two pairs of gloves and a cap with ear flaps. Grabbing a snow shovel, he headed out into the bitter wind that was still laced with snow crystals.

Meanwhile, back in the house, Mom decided it was a good day for the girls to do some extra dusting. A couple of batches of cookies and cinnamon rolls would be good. The men would need something warm when they came in for a break. Milk for hot cocoa warmed on the back burner of the cook stove.

There were no snow blowers then, so while Delmer shoveled by hand, Dad and Don spent most of a Snow Day on the cabless tractor, using the loader to scoop snow and haul it to growing piles. The yard had to be cleared for vehicles. The cattle needed open space to eat hay and a walkway to the feeders.

Delmer with his trusty shovel scooped snow to create paths to the hen-house and all the outbuildings. He cleared openings to the barnyard gates and made the doorways accessible for chores. After a few hours, fingers feeling frozen and arms and back aching, the boy wondered why he had been so happy that morning over a Snow Day. By three o'clock that afternoon, feet and shovel dragging, my brother was thinking maybe he would rather be in school.

MOM'S HOT COCOA

1 cup sugar
2/3 cup unsweetened cocoa powder
9 cups top milk
1 tsp vanilla

In large kettle, combine sugar, cocoa and 1 cup milk. Stir constantly over medium heat until mixture comes to a boil Cook, stirring constantly for 2 minutes. Add remaining milk and heat, but do not boil. Remove from heat and stir in vanilla.

Serve hot with marshmallows.

Christmas Story: The Scene in the Snow Globe

A thick flurry of flakes churns and swirls wildly, creating a crystalline wall of white. Gradually, the whirling slows and the gossamer flecks begin to drift and flutter gently, magically revealing a snow globe scene.

A little girl, hands clasped at her heart, gazes up at the tree in the corner of the small living room. She and her younger brother stand sheltered between Mom and Dad. Their eyes reflect the dazzling lights that flicker before them, melding the colors and textures into a beautiful Christmas memory. The idyllic image glows in my mind as I envision my sister's remembrances of an enchanting night long, long ago.

It was the girl's fourth Christmas. The warm scents of spruce and burning wax mingled together as the day's events flashed through her mind. As Dad headed out the door that morning, bundled in his winter coveralls and cap and overshoes, he had turned to Mom and said quietly. "We have to give them a Christmas."

Later Mom popped a huge bowl of popcorn. With Don in his high chair, tasting bits of the white fluff, Deloris and Mom used darning needles to string the popped kernels and bright red cranberries into a long rope. That afternoon Dad tugged a small tree in through the kitchen. Mom brought a coffee can filled with wet sand, and together they set the tree in its stand of bright wooden pine boards. "We can't let the tree dry out," Dad said as they worked. "There was another fire near Brookings. They lost…" He paused and glanced at the children as they looked up at him, waiting. Then he ruffled Don's blond hair and smiled wistfully. "Let's get this tree decorated!"

Dad held his small boy up close to the top and helped the pudgy little hands nestle the star into the branches. Mom had cut a star out of a box and covered it with precious tin foil. They wrapped the popcorn-cranberry garland all around the tree. Then the children helped drape "icicles" over the tips of the branches. Mom had saved the tinsel from last year, carefully laying each strand on a piece of cardboard, then wrapping all in newspaper.

When the silver strings covered the tree, Dad brought out the box of candles and burnished brass candle holders. Mom smiled. "We used these on our Christmas trees when I was growing up." She carefully pushed a white candle into each holder, and Dad began clipping them onto branches.

Soon twenty-four small white pillars stood out against the dark green needles. Mom left for a few minutes and came back carrying two small packages wrapped in white tissue paper. She placed them under the tree.

The regal spruce stood solemnly, as though it knew how important it was on this special Christmas Day. "Are you ready?" Dad asked the girl and boy as he used a match to light a stubby red candle that was waxed unto a plate. "Mom and I will light the candles. Then we'll turn out the lantern. The candles can burn for just a little while." Two little heads looked up in wonder and solemnly nodded.

Again the snow globe picture glitters in my mind—the family standing before their tree, the light of the candles glowing in the darkness. Like icicles touched by first rays of sunlight, the tinsel shimmers in reply. They sing Silent Night.

With hands crossed over her heart, the little girl stares at the glorious sight. The reflection of the light glows in her eyes, and those of her little brother, her mother and her father. A portrait is etched in their hearts as a precious memory that comes back to life as the story flows from the Nooks and Crannies of my sister's mind.

Those were simpler times. No electricity. No layers of gifts were piled under the tree. But the joy and hope shined as brightly as the candles on that spruce so long ago, encircled in light and love, like a snow globe.

I wish you a snow globe Christmas.

☀

The Mystery of the Little Green Snowsuit

My sister's eyes shone as she unpacked the last item from the box of outgrown baby things she had brought to share. "Oh, DeAnn, this was yours!" She held up a small pastel-green snowsuit. It was made from tightly woven nylon. Stretchy ribbed cuffs kept out the snow and cold on the sleeves and legs. Elastic encircled the waist. Sewn inside was a white crepe, quilted lining. A sturdy zipper ran from the collar all the way down to the bottom cuff of the left leg. The small garment was still in good shape, even after being handed down to five more children.

Thoughtfully, I ran my fingers over the snowsuit. The fabric rustled softly. I could not help but wonder why my parents would have purchased such a frivolous thing. They grew up during the Depression; the "waste not, want not" philosophy was engrained in them. Why did they spend hard-earned money on a suit that their one-year-old toddler would wear (outside and for "everyday") for only a few months?

Of course I did not remember wearing the snowsuit those twenty-some years back, but drifting from the nooks and crannies of my mind there was a photo…

Psychologists claim we begin to remember events as early as the age of two but much more so after seven. Every one of my siblings remembers our growing-up experiences in the South Dakota winter wonderland.

Whether whirling and twirling or plopping ponderously on our posteriors, ice skating rated high on our list of winter sport. Deloris and Dorothy reminisce of the years when we had our personal skating strip just south of the house. Fall rains sometimes filled the ditch and frigid temps turned the pond into frozen glass. It didn't matter if we had to shovel it off first. Even that could be done on skates. A few miles away, Spirit Lake provided an ice rink along the shore almost every year. If we were lucky, we could skate nearby as Mom and Dad sat around their fishing holes.

My first skates each had two blades and three leather straps that attached to my boots. No figure-eights at that age, but I couldn't wait to graduate to white leather shoe skates with single blades (and puffy black pompoms with bells). Pompoms were rather posh for the frozen stock dam, but it was within walking distance and the cows didn't mind much. Delmer recollects playing hockey with the neighbor kids until all hours of the night, with rules tweaked just slightly. Or, what could be more fun than a game of Kick-the-Can on the ice under a bright December moon?

Some winters, wild winds deposited deep drifts just outside the house. Delmer and I scooped out tunnels and snow shelters that even Rex found cozy. They proved to be good cover when Dad and Don itched for a snowball fight. Don waited with the patience of Job until we dared peek around the corner. Dad laughed hysterically when his snowball caught us unawares.

Dad contrived some interesting devices for sledding. Darlene and Dorothy remember riding in an old car hood that Dad pulled behind the John Deere 520. We all fit on "The Tin," the all-purpose farm implement that he made by bolting two strips of the soft metal together and attaching a chain. Behind the tractor the five-by-ten-foot piece of flat metal glided over snow and ice around the buildings and through the yard, while we hung on for dear life, screaming with delight.

Sometimes storms filled the driveway with massive drifts of white that needed to be moved. Dad used his tractor and loader to scoop snow into a 15-foot pile, strategically placed for speed and distance. The thrill of victory was strong when we skidded all the way to the barn. Then we dragged the old wooden sled with thin metal runners back up the mountain and flew down again and again. I remember a time or two when our mother even took on the sled challenge, grinning all the way down.

More than fifty years later as I write this story, I have before me a well-worn green snowsuit and a black and white photograph. The snowsuit rustles softly as I rest my hand on it. I gaze at the picture. There on the wooden sled with runners sits three children. A young boy in front, an older girl in the back, and snug in the middle, a toddler in a snowsuit. Our faces are beaming with happy smiles as bright as the winter sun.

Now I know why Mom and Dad bought the snowsuit. They bought it for fun.

☀

When the Table Is Turned

In the mid-fifties Dad and Don lugged our round oak kitchen table out to the barn and replaced it with a shiny new Art Deco model. The decade was the era of post-war abundance. As with hemlines and cars, Americans wanted their kitchens up-to-date. Style called for bright and bold, and the table was the most prominent piece of furniture in the room.

Ours had shiny chrome legs and frame and a four-inch apron all around the edge. It was a rectangle with rounded corners. The top gleamed with a gray and white marble Formica.

The youngest of six, this was the only kitchen table I remember as I grew up on our South Dakota farm.

Besides providing a gathering place for every meal and snack, the table was the heart of activity for children and adults. Bread raised and cookies cooled on it. Mom and Dad scaled and cleaned the latest catch of fish. Garden peas plopped into bowls as we sat next to the table, and we tossed the crunchy pods into buckets awaiting under it. Young hands performed surgery on small appliances; sometimes all the pieces even fit back together.

Company came and gravitated to the table. Quietly it witnessed laughter and tears. The hub of the kitchen was a desk for paying bills and for six youngsters to do homework, sometimes all gathered around at once.

The chrome-festooned table was the home for countless activities all week long, but on Friday nights when the dishes were done the practical kitchen table transformed like magic. It turned into the stage for our own indoor winter Olympics. Let the games begin!

With a paddle at each corner and a short green net attached to the center of the table, soon ping pong balls were flying. Occasionally we got a little vigorous and one landed in the wash sink or bounced off the curved glass of Mom's precious china cabinet. (We held our breath.) At least once the sphere soared to the top of the hot cook stove. Sisters set speed records to save the plastic ball from a meltdown. Meanwhile, our mother sat in the next room, mostly unaware of the wild warfare in the kitchen. This was good, as we could usually talk her into picking up a paddle later in the competition.

We learned to shuffle cards at a very young age. Nothing like Slap Jack to hone focus and reaction skills. I pestered Dad until he played Old Maid.

Almost always, with feigned remorse he announced to Mom, "I am the Old Maid AGAIN." The older siblings taught us younger ones to play Rattle and Rummy, then took great pleasure in trouncing us.

Every board game of the time stood by, ready to be pulled out of the metal storage cabinet in the upstairs bathroom. Yahtzee, Skunk, Checkers, Uno, Scrabble. If Mom offered prizes someone volunteered to call the Bingo numbers. The more cards we played, the better chance for a win, right? Corn made great markers, and if a few kernels flew off the table, we could just sweep the floor later!

Dad bought a wooden Carrom board on a farm sale. The kitchen became a mini-pool room as we mastered the art. The red and black rings zoomed across the board, occasionally into the intended mesh pockets. The most difficult shots required bouncing the shooter off the opponent's side to knock in a ring close to your own side.

When I was four I got a Cootie game for Christmas. Delmer, being the good sport that he was (sometimes), conceded to play. There was much eye rolling and gnashing of teeth on my brother's part as, with the luck of the roll, I completed my bug first. He evened the score years later when our elbows rested on the table next to the Monopoly game. Somehow, I always managed to go directly to jail while he accumulated houses, hotels and railroads. It was 2:00 AM and I was really tired. You would be tired, too, if you were suffering the same agony of defeat! But he made me stay to the bitter end, broke and dejected.

Next morning the table was turned back to its original everyday business. We poured milk on our Cheerios. "I sure had fun playing Monopoly last night," my brother said with a satisfied smirk. Of course he did, and he had to rub it in.

I shrugged nonchalantly as if it meant nothing to me. But secretly, I was planning my game strategy. I couldn't wait until next Friday night when the table was turned.

When Green Was Just a Color

"We don't want it to go to waste." Our mother said it. She lived it. She taught it to her family. During our growing up years when we were saving, stretching, repairing, reusing and repurposing, we had no idea that we were using environmentally-friendly practices; the "green" movement had not yet begun. It was simply the way we lived.

Our parents grew up during the Depression. Our grandparents lived through the Great War. They all experienced the rationing of World War II. Frugal living was in their blood, and they passed it on to our generation.

We saved. When cotton string was sewn into the tops of flour sacks or paper bags, we gently pulled it out and later wound it around the ball of saved string that waited in the pencil drawer. You never knew when you might need string! The same went for scraps of fabric and slips of paper. We trimmed the blank area from the backs of cards and envelopes. The good thing about all this saving was that we always had craft materials available for important projects.

Slivers of soap stuck to the new bar if "glued" on with plenty of suds and left to dry. Old catalogs were carried to the outhouse where they were used for---um, reading material, of course!

Kleenex and paper towels beckoned from grocery shelves, but why buy something, use it once and just throw it away? Handkerchiefs and rags served the same purposes quite nicely.

Salvaged sections of baling wire saved the day many times when strategically stashed under pickup and tractor seats or on a nail in the Quonset. Delmer and Don spent an occasional afternoon with a hammer and cement block. They pounded bent nails to straighten them and tossed them into an old paint can, ready for use.

In the kitchen we used the waxed paper liners in cereal boxes for packing sandwiches. When split down the side they served as cooling sheets for bread and cookies. Tin foil was washed and used over and over again. Re-using the old saved on purchasing new. Egg shells were dried in an old oatmeal canister, to be crushed later and fed to the chickens or the tomato plants in the garden. The chickens loved fruit and vegetable peels. The dog and barn cats feasted on meat scraps. Bacon grease flavored fried eggs and potatoes wonderfully. "Potato water," the liquid drained from the cooked vegetable, added flavor and nutrients to gravy and homemade bread.

No gift bags back then, but we carefully folded and packed away the larger pieces of used wrapping paper, especially at Christmas, and we kept a handy stash of ribbons and bows to use again and again.

Small jars which had held olives or maraschino cherries made great jelly jars. Mom filled them with chokecherry or apple and sealed them with melted paraffin. When we opened the jar, we removed the solid circle of wax on top and stored it with the others in a blue porcelain cup for use again next year.

I don't remember being told I had to clean up my plate at mealtimes, but I did know that if there were vegetables and meat remaining on it, I had better not count on dessert! Like everything else, food was not to be wasted.

Our mother mended and patched clothes until they were too thin to patch. Then my sisters and I helped her cut off the buttons and rip out zippers and elastic to be used again to repair another garment. What was left was salvaged for rugs or tossed into the rag drawer. I remember Mom sitting in her chair after supper and darning socks. She pushed a lightbulb into the heal or toe of the sock, wherever the hole was. Then she used her darning needle to weave thread into a curved patch over the hole. The mend was so smooth that the big toe did not even notice it.

We all worked together on our South Dakota farm. We fixed and saved and reused everything possible. Though our motto at the time was closer to "A penny saved" than "Go green," we still conserved trees and other resources and kept trash to a minimum. The things we did were small things, but cumulatively they made a difference, because "Every little bit helps!" Our mom said that, too.

☀

Rock and Roll

Dinner warmed on the back burner of the cook stove. Potato soup left from last night's supper. And there was fresh bread. Though her husband was late, she waited to eat with him. He would need a hot meal after standing in the cold at the auction sale. Another family selling out and moving away. The hardships of the thirties were still taking their toll even though the Depression was over.

She heard the old Ford pickup rumble into the driveway and hurried to the frigid porch to open the door. He lifted a large basket-like object over the step and maneuvered it into the porch and the kitchen. Gently, he set the four-wheels on the floor and pushed the metal handle forward.

The woman's eyes lit with a smile as she ran her fingers over the sturdy willow strands of the wicker baby buggy. A hinged hood swiveled up or down over the head of the bed. The entire wicker unit hung suspended on inch-wide metal strips, allowing a rocking movement that occurred both when the buggy rolled forward and when it stood at rest. Two eight-inch round windows on the hood allowed quick peeks from the side. She had no idea then how useful those little portholes would be in the years ahead.

The next afternoon she sewed a new cushion and hemmed soft flannel sheets for the buggy which waited in the living room, just around the corner. In less than three months the couple tenderly tucked their first child into the soft warm buggy.

The new mother learned to work fast when the baby slept, running outside to water the chickens or gather the eggs or turn on the windmill, then racing back in the house to listen intently for the tiny girl's cry. The mom scrambled to do the baking and put meals on the table. Sometimes she managed a few minutes in her chair next to the buggy. With gentle rocking of the carriage and a soft lullaby, the little one would again drift into her dreams.

Deloris grew and thrived and became Mommy's little helper when a tiny new brother arrived and was lovingly tucked into his daytime bed, the wicker buggy. Two little ones to care for presented far more than twice the work, but Mom and Dad took it all in stride. Though barely nineteen months old, Deloris learned to nudge the baby bed back and forth to soothe Donald's fussing. One afternoon, Mom scrubbed carrots and potatoes in the kitchen sink while Deloris played in the next room near the carriage. Suddenly, the house seemed too quiet and Mom peeked around the corner. Deloris had climbed into the buggy, and taking her mommy's helper role very seriously, she was trying to pick Donald up and lift him out. Mom did not make a sound for fear of startling the girl but rushed to rescue her son, who happily grinned at both of them.

Time went on and the wicker buggy served its purpose well. Two more daughters, Darlene and Dorothy, took their turns napping, often with their older sister at the wheels. Then came a baby boy who had several older sisters to entertain him. Delmer quickly outgrew the wicker bed and began his farming operation in the sandbox.

At last, Mom and Dad brought a sixth baby home from the hospital. Within a month her crooked little grin and mischievous eyes worked in her favor as she passed Manipulation 101 with flying colors. Dorothy, barely eight, was often assigned the rock-and-roll-the-baby job. At first, she managed to get in plenty of precious play time as soon as the baby dozed off, but soon the task grew more difficult. One afternoon, she really wanted to play with her dolls. Mom had sewn three new doll dresses and Dorothy couldn't wait to try them on. She cradled her doll in her right arm while she kept the woven basket in motion with her left. At last, after continuing for what seemed like hours, she stopped rocking. Waited. Listened. Released a deep breath. Relieved at her

(Dorothy Holter)

apparent success at getting her baby sister to sleep, she stood to dash to the box of doll clothes. But wait! What was that noise? Dorothy groaned and clapped her hand to her forehead. Inside the buggy, DeAnn lifted her head and peeked through the round window, right at her big sister---and giggled! The young girl's blond pigtails shook in dismay as she rolled her eyes and sighed dramatically. Longingly, she stared at the doll dresses across the room. She rocked the buggy some more.

The trusty wicker buggy remains in our family today, a reminder of all the babies who napped (or not) in our South Dakota farm living room. It is ironic that it now proudly rests in my sister Dorothy's guest room. Her precious baby doll can be seen if you peek through the portholes.

I do not recall my time spent in the old buggy. From my siblings' stories I imagine....sisters set on getting the baby to sleep so they could do their own thing. Rocking. Waiting. Hoping. Then I think of mischievously peeking out at them through the little porthole---and I can't help but giggle!

The Book Report: Ode to the Manual Typewriter

I was drying supper dishes and made the mistake of mentioning to Mom that I had a book report due tomorrow. Actually, the report was done; I just needed to type it. She offered to finish dishes. I declined and rationalized my procrastination with a touch of teenage drama. "Life is short, Mom. What if I died in my sleep tonight? Wouldn't you be happier knowing I had not spent my last earthly moments tortured by a typewriter?"

She replied something about me looking pretty healthy, then added that in heaven God probably required Good Book Reports. I didn't tell her that I was thinking that typewriters more likely came from the depths of the other place. She must have read my mind because she lifted the kettle and dish towel from my hands and pointed to the table, the homework spot. My moment of reckoning had come!

With a huge sigh, I gathered the needed materials. My assignment notebook. The written copy of my report. A tablet of typing paper. A package of white-coated "Correct-It" squares. A typing eraser with a plastic brush on the end. Carbon paper.

I lugged the typewriter into the kitchen from the closet. Years back we had a bigger machine, a Royal. My older sisters won speed-typing competitions with it at college.

I plopped the case on the table with a bit more force than necessary, opened it, undid the locking clips and set it out on the Formica surface. I stared at the blue Smith Corona with four rows of keys and a long space bar, all attached to individual metal rods underneath. I looked inside to see the rows of arms that waited until you pushed down their key, then they slapped against the ink-filled ribbon and printed that letter. On the left a chrome lever with a finger indent protruded from the carriage which held the rollers. The carriage moved to the left as you typed. A bell dinged near the end of the line. You had to reach up with your left hand and push the lever all the way to the right which returned the carriage back to the beginning of the next line.

I might as well get started. It wasn't like I could talk to it and it would type what I said. Wouldn't that be something?

A quick glance through my book report notes: At least two type-written pages, double-spaced with standard margins. Points deducted for errors. Carbon copy required.

I tore two sheets of typing paper off the tablet and placed a flimsy carbon sheet between them. Last time I had put the carbon paper in wrong-side-down and the only "copy" was the backwards clone of my science report on its back. I considered not retyping it and telling Mr. Cheadle he could read it by holding it up to a mirror, but decided I needed to pass science.

Using a folded sheet of paper to keep the three sheets in line, I turned the knob on the rollers. I lined up the papers with margins and typed the class name, etc. in the left corner.

The title needed to be centered. I counted the letters and spaces in The Last of the Mohicans. Twenty-four. I set the carriage to the exact center of the page and clicked the backspace key twelve times. Typed the title. Same procedure with the author. James Fenimore Cooper? Couldn't someone invent an easier way to center a line? I made a mental note to read a book by an author with a short name for my next book report.

Main characters. Setting. Plot. Handwritten copy ready, I started typing. My fingers were moving along and I caught the rhythm as I transferred the words to the paper, line by line. Click, clack, click. Ding. Zzziiippp! Getting the hang of it, I began thinking maybe this typing stuff was not so bad. Just then I glanced up. I had forgotten to set the carriage return to double space. I stared at the crowded words for a second and then ripped the papers up through the top of the rollers.

The second time progressed faster and I remembered to double space. Again, I clicked along fairly fast. All at once something did not seem right. I had forgotten the paragraph indent. Too much to erase.

The fifth restart was finally getting along when the bell dinged and I kept going, pushing to get the whole word in the line. It would not fit. I could not divide "trappers" before the "e" so I used the correcting tape. Holding it next to the paper I typed over the letters to cover them with white.

Two hours later I pelted out the final words and rolled the papers free. Rats! I had an extra "e" at the end of "Hawkeye." Papers back in the machine, I tried to set the line on the exact same place to type over with the correcting tape. Not possible. I grabbed the eraser…

At last, I separated the three layers of each page and stapled the two copies. Seven large smoke puffs smudged the carbons. On the teacher's copy was only one small hole where the eraser wore through.

Picking up the crumpled papers dispersed throughout the kitchen, I thought of my next assignment, a research paper with footnotes. I closed the cover on the case. Hopefully, SOMEDAY someone will invent a better machine, one that will correct mistakes. Wouldn't that be something?

Hats ON! Imagination Inspiration

The Golden Age of Millinery was nearing the end of its sparkle when I was born in the fifties. Headdress as fashion began during the Industrial Revolution and continued through mid-twentieth century. In the Nooks and Crannies of my mind my mother loved hats. Dad would tell her to buy a new one, often for Easter. This was one of the few luxuries she allowed herself during the years she and Dad raised six children.

When women dressed up during that era, they stepped into heels, then crowned their heads with the finishing touch before they glanced in the mirror and walked out the door. Every special occasion required a hat, but mostly I remember them in church.

Our family often sat in the same pew, close to the back at our little country church, West Bethany Lutheran. Don ushered and the older girls helped with music, so just four of us filed in this one particular Sunday. I sat on the far end next to Mom. Delmer sat soberly between Mom and Dad. Ever since he had made that parting comment to the pastor as we shook hands and exited the church, the folks felt the need to guard him. I did not understand what was so terrible about it. My brother had simply grinned up at the minister and bid him good-bye. So an alligator was mentioned. It was just a kid's popular farewell message. The additional statement that included a timeline for straighter teeth—well, I suppose it could have been misconstrued as an insult, but it showed creativity and imagination on my brother's part, as well as rhyming skills. Needless to say, Dad and Mom did not appreciate his talents at the time.

Mom in one of her hats.
(Dorothy Holter)

So there I was feeling bad for my brother who hardly dared move. Dad stared straight ahead, probably hoping his kids would not embarrass him today. I looked up at Mom and took in her hat. It was a green silk brocade with golden threads outlining flower petals. A narrow brim surrounded it at a slight angle. A matching velvet ribbon circled just above the brim. On the front a round pendant sparkled like emeralds on the ribbon.

Just then the pastor stepped into the pulpit. I always had a vivid imagination and at a very young age I discovered that it was the most active at two definite times: One, racing back to the house in pitch dark after closing for the chickens, and two, sitting quietly in a church pew---during the sermon.

So, all that sermonizing inspired my brain into high gear. I looked around to see if any other women's hats were as pretty as Mom's.

The nice pianist wore a navy-blue satin; Mother called it a pillbox. Immediately, I imagined tiny white tablets spilling out as her fingers pounded the keys. My sisters said the First Lady often wore a pillbox. Who was the First Lady? From the background of my mind, the pastor's reading from Genesis trickled into my image. That's it! Eve was the first lady. My short legs began swinging back and forth in excitement. Mom gave me "the look." My legs stopped. But, wait a minute. Why would Eve have bothered with a hat?

My gaze wandered to three ladies in the front pew who waited to sing the special music. Their hats fit close to their heads like wide headbands. One was white lace. The middle hat sparkled with brown sequins. A purple bow bent over the short gray curls of the third. Three arches of color swayed slightly in rhythm with the lesson. Vaguely words from Matthew, something about "birds of the air," fluttered from the front. All at once, I imagined three wild geese flying in formation, their honking fading into the distance.

On the other side of the church a beautiful image of a rooster pheasant flashed into my mind. I saw him rise into the air, chirping his flight call. The hat that inspired my vision curved over the lady's head like an upside-down bowl covered with feathers. One long tail feather skimmed the side. I felt sorry for the pheasant.

In the row directly in front of me a white net drooped to gray-sleeved shoulders. The netting circled all around in front of the girl's eyes. Something about Paul and locusts and wild honey droned in from the pulpit area. All at once a terrific idea buzzed into my brain! That veil was the perfect protection from the bees and wasps that sometimes circled above the sanctuary as if deciding who to dive-bomb next. My feet started moving again.

My mother released a sigh of relief as "Amen" resounded through the building. The sermon was over.

I followed Delmer as we filed out past the preacher. He politely shook the man's hand and moved on. I nodded, barely touched the outstretched hand and rushed out the door. I could not look up at the guy in robes because I knew I would check to see if the "alligator's" teeth were any straighter.

On the five-mile-drive home Dad glanced in the rearview mirror and addressed Delmer. "You sat real nice in church today, Son." I felt a bit miffed that he did not comment on my exemplary behavior.

Then our father started reviewing the main points of the sermon. I blinked up at my mom's pretty hat. Suddenly my eyes glazed over and I turned to the window. I scanned the sky for flying geese.

☼

The Best Part of Having a Haymow

"Make sure Mama Kitty gets plenty to eat. She's looking pretty thin," Dad instructed me one afternoon in late March. I stared at the floor for a moment. She was not thin last night when I fed all the cats.

Growing up on our South Dakota farm we learned about the birds and the bees at an early age. Storks and pumpkin seeds? We knew better! So if the mother cat was suddenly skinny, it could mean only one thing.

The folks always told us to leave baby kittens alone or the mother cat would move them. I knew they would not approve of me climbing up into the haymow, so later that day when Mom was in the chicken coop and the men were doing hog chores, I slipped into the middle door of the barn.

Our haymow (rhymes with cow) covered the whole barn and served as a storage place for bales of alfalfa, brome hay and straw which were stacked in the middle. When needed, we dropped the feed or bedding to the live-stock below through strategic openings in the floor.

I gazed up at the three one-by-four boards that were nailed across the barn framework and served as the ladder to the upper level. The boards were spaced for legs much longer than mine, but I managed to pull myself up to the first one and then one-step the rest of the way. At last I scrambled onto

the rough wooden floor boards. A light switch hugged the side of the ladder post. I flipped the switch and a huge room emerged from the darkness.

Dust motes danced through the light above. The musty smell of hay and straw blended with the animal odors from below. My breath rose, a cloud of steam in the cold air.

I scanned the area for a potential pediatric ward. A small pile of bales remained in the center of the room. In the far corner where the barn roof curved down and the space narrowed, a few old bales remained from previous years. Thick blankets of cobwebs drooped from the ceiling to the hay. As I moved closer, I heard a tiny mew.

In a triangular opening Mama Kitty sat with her tail curled around her. She looked up at me as I peeked over the bale, then went about the bathing-the-babies business. Her rough tongue lifted the kitten bodies off their straw bed. I watched in fascination as tiny heads bobbed about searching for Mother. Eyes shut, they mewed and tumbled over each other, finally finding nourishment. Purr button on high, Mama Kitty lay down, stretched out and closed her eyes. I reached in and petted her soft gray head. Then I rubbed one finger between the bitty ears of a kitten.

Suddenly I heard scuffing noises as someone climbed up the vertical ladder. I was miffed that I would have to share the secret of the baby kittens, and I figured he would tell.

My brother Delmer sidled up next to the old bales. "How many does she have?"

"Four."

"How old are they?"

"Just born last night." For several minutes we reveled in the scene. Then my brother glanced up at the spider webs. He said it was a good thing the old bales were still there for the kittens. A couple years ago a distinct odor of skunk kept anyone from moving the bales. Then no one wanted to tear into the webs, so the old hay remained.

"The good hay will be gone in a couple weeks," he said as he got up to toss down feed. "Then Don and I will sweep it out and play ball up here. It's the best part of having a haymow."

He carried a bale and I rolled one over to the opening above the bull's pen. Pushing one knee into it, he pulled off the twine and tossed chunks of hay down the opening. I stepped right next to the edge of the hole and looked down. My stomach lurched as I saw two pairs of curled horns twist about as the Hereford bulls tore off tufts of hay. Then Delmer told me about last spring when he and Don had been bouncing the basketball against the haymow wall. It had rolled down into the bull enclosure. He had to go down below and rescue the ball. My stomach lurched again.

We moved to the south side and dropped two straw bales. My brother tossed off his coat as sweat beaded on his forehead. He and Don had sweated plenty when they filled the haymow last summer. Not a breath of air stirred in the room above the barn on the hottest day of the year. They brought a load of bales from the field and unloaded them onto the elevator that carried them up through the big door on the front of the barn. Then they stacked them again, ready for winter feed and bedding.

Delmer finished chores in the haymow, and I followed him down the ladder.

That night at supper Dad asked if I was feeding Mama Kitty. I nodded. "Yup, I'm taking good care of her." I sneaked a glance at Delmer, but he didn't say a word.

The next night when Mom was in the chicken coop, and the guys were doing hog chores, I slipped into the barn....I peeked over the old bales. I watched the miracle before me and I knew for certain---THIS was the best part of having a haymow.

The Direct Connection Revealed

A dusting of white coated the front of her apron. Tiny flecks of flour puffed into the air as her arms moved back and forth over the table. Soft brushing sounds followed gentle thumps as the rolling pin descended and the handles turned within her fingers, flattening the dough slightly with each pass. Her head bobbed lightly to the beat of her work and the hymn she hummed, "Blest be the tie that binds…" All the while a smile beamed on her face.

Mom lifted the circle of dough from the board, sprinkled flour in the center and continued the rolling process. When it was big enough, she folded it, settled it into the pie plate, and then opened it again, the edges drooping slightly over the glass rim. She repeated the process with the top crust, cutting small slits in the folds.

The filling cooled on the stove, sour cream raisin; it was Dad's favorite. As she poured it into the bottom crust, a warm spicy aroma rose with the steam. She unfolded the top crust and lowered it onto the filling. With a practiced touch she turned the pie around, both hands pressing around the edge to seal and score. A paring knife made quick work of the excess dough, which she tossed back into the bowl for the next pie. Then she fluted the edges. Two fingers pressed down with her right hand while the index finger of her left hand pushed up the dough between them, all around the edge. A perfect pattern of ridges and valleys quickly framed her work and sealed the two crusts. She sprinkled a handful of sugar over the top. It sparkled as she carried the pie to the oven.

As she reached for her rolling pin to prepare another crust, the woman's

thoughts traveled back to when she and Dad were married. She followed her own mother's tradition of baking on Saturday, presenting the flaky-crusted dessert for every Sunday dinner. It seemed like only yesterday.

Many years had passed, many pies prepared, and their six children had grown up. Some lived far away and could visit only once or twice a year, but some lived close by. More often than not, when Mom knew someone was stopping in, she got out her rolling pin.

Christmas meant sugar cookies and raisin-filled cookies and of course, lefse. That rolling cylinder put in a lot of miles in Mom's hands as she prepared for the holidays. Sometimes Dad or one of the girls helped. No matter how much work was involved, when Mom was using her rolling pin, she was smiling.

Months later when snow blanketed the garden, she stirred and kneaded a batch of sweet dough. As it rose on the back of the stove, she brought out the rolling pin. With floured donut cutters, Mom soon had cookie sheets loaded with rising donuts and centers. We felt like royalty when we walked in the door and were greeted with the aroma of fresh glazed donuts.

On another cold day the handy rolling pin smoothed a similar dough into a rectangle. Mom spread on butter and sprinkled a generous layer of cinnamon and sugar. She happily rolled the rectangle into a thick rope, sliced it in sections and tucked them into a cake pan to rise. In two hours, warm, flaky rolls, dripping with frosting adorned an etched glass plate in the center of the table. Oh, my. I think even the angels were singing.

Mom's rolling pin played a part in many more heavenly delights, and now I see there was a pattern established. When our mother got out her rolling pin, some quite complicated culinary delight was about to happen. Always, it involved time and work. Always, it was a gift for someone she loved. Always, she smiled when it moved between her hands.

Cherished memories flow from the Nooks and Crannies of my mind today as I study Mom's precious rolling pin before me. I brush my fingers over the wooden cylinder and think of the thousands of turns it made, guided by her hands. The heavy maple is still smooth after 80 years, the streaks running through it like a river that goes on forever. The handles, shaped perfectly to roll between fingers, sport a few dents and scratches, but they are sturdy, ready to work.

I picture my mother as she stood at the kitchen table, canisters of flour and sugar arranged alongside a big bowl of dough. The rolling pin waits-- for both of us. I lift it by the cylinder as she would have and lower it to the table. Then I place one hand on each handle and push gently forward. The roller turns within my fingers and suddenly an amazing awareness floods through my soul. Mom's rolling pin joins my hands to my heart. A direct connection. Now I know why my mother smiled.

"Make Hay While the Sun Shines"

We did. Almost every summer the relentless sun beat down, "hotter than a pistol," especially on haying days. Whether out in the hayfield, at the top of a stack or in the sweltering haymow, the memories of putting up hay that flow from the nooks and crannies of my siblings' minds often include the words "hot and sweaty."

A sense of urgency loomed over our father during spring planting, fall harvest and summer haying. He and Mom grew up in lean years and now carried the responsibility of eight mouths to feed, so when their livelihood was on the line, the demands on himself and his family were high. Most often, we stepped up to the plate and powered through. Once in a while, though, expectations exceeded human and mechanical limits, and the results were disastrous.

Dad's first baler was a wire-tie, John Deere (of course). My brother Delmer tells me that by the time he and I were old enough to help, the wire baler had been replaced by a twine-tie. Since the wire fasteners allowed more hay to be packed in to each bale (a hundred pounds or more!), Delmer adds that we were fortunate in that respect.

The first twine developed for balers was a natural fiber. Not nearly as strong as wire, the sisal sometimes broke; busted bales dotted the hayfield. These needed to be picked up by hand and tossed into the pickup or re-baled. Mice merrily munched on the ties, resulting in more loose bundles in the stacks or haymow. Soon plastic replaced the natural fiber ties. Nylon strings did not often break, but sometimes the smooth knots did not hold.

No matter the machine, on our farm Dad did the mowing and baling. Plentiful rainfall occasionally provided three cuttings of alfalfa, but South Dakota weather did not always make life easy. Some years we were lucky to have two cuttings and even those were sparse. During drought years, Dad cut the strip of grass next to the shelter belt. The sweet smell of brome mingled with the pungent alfalfa in the haymow. A couple seasons when no rains came, our father cut the reed canary grass in the slough, much like Pa Ingalls and Almanzo in The Long Winter.

Bales required picking up and hauling. Mom, Donald, sometimes the older girls, and eventually, Delmer and I worked into the hay scene. In the field, like a train engine pulling cars, the tractor pulled the bale loader and the hay rack. Bales traveled up the loader and pushed out onto the rack where one or two strong-backed workers stacked the bales, packing in as many as possible to be hauled home. There they had to be unloaded and piled again into one of several stacks that served as livestock feed for the winter.

In bountiful years, when the baler cranked out tons of bales in a short space, my sisters and I walked through the field and pulled the meandering, bound bundles into a straight row. This made the job easier for the tractor driver, who had to guide the arm on the loader right next to the bale so it would follow up the chains and plop onto the rack behind. Mom and Darlene quickly mastered the driving technique, then Delmer took over at a very young age.

One hot, sunny August afternoon Don and Dad rode on the rack. Delmer, barely eleven, drove the John Deere 730 through the alfalfa field, maneuvering each bale into the loader. The men stacked the bales on the flatbed until it was full, then hauled them home. The pile in the barnyard grew taller with each load as the day wore on. An ominous dark bank threatened in the western horizon as Delmer drove down the last row of bales. A quick glance back revealed that the rack was full. He eased up on the throttle and gently pulled the clutch, bringing the tractor to a stop. The boy waited for instructions. Dad jabbed his bale hook into the nearest block of hay, pulled the red bandanna out of his back pocket and wiped the sweat from his eyes. He took in the jam-packed pile behind him, then silently counted the bales that remained. Finally, Dad motioned to Delmer to keep going. They would try to get all the bales on this load.

Donald tugged at his leather gloves and stared up at the top of the stack. He shook his head. Delmer took a deep breath and pushed the clutch gently forward, intent on getting the job done. He focused steadily on steering each bale directly into the loader. Don climbed. Dad lifted. No one noticed the gaping badger hole as the tractor tire sidled past it. Suddenly, the right front wheel of the heavy-laden flatbed dropped into the hole. A loud crack ripped through the air as the rack jerked to a halt. Bales tumbled from the top and side of the mountain, creating a tangled wreckage on the stubble below.

Two hours later, after driving home and returning to the field with jacks and wheel repair parts, then adding muscle, pounding and prayers, they were ready to go again. Back on the tractor, Delmer eased the flatbed over the filled-in hole and moved forward.

Later, as the haying crew turned toward home, the threatening black cloud smothered the warm rays of sunshine and the sky grew dark.

Did they manage to get all the bales on that last load? What do YOU think?

No Matter What, We Had to Try

Life seldom goes as planned. Bad timing. Unintentional disaster. Mother Nature unleashing her mighty powers. We have all come upon animals in a bad situation, but animal rescues were simply part of life as we grew up on our South Dakota farm.

Though livestock births were usually planned to occur in warm spring weather, every year a calf or lamb decided to enter the world early. Combine that with harsh weather and a first-time mother's desire for privacy, and the result was often a perilous beginning for a vulnerable new life.

Dad and Don checked the flock every evening as they threw hay over the fence. One February night a ewe was missing. The frigid South Dakota wind whipped at the new snow, creating a ground blizzard. They could barely see the small cluster of trees that grew next to the frozen pond, but they trudged painstakingly through the pasture, searching for the lost sheep. Their five-buckle overshoes sank into deep drifts as the wind drove frost-laden flecks into their watchful eyes. Finally, Don spotted a dark shape against a white backdrop. The black-faced sheep lay in front of a drift under the bare limbs of an old ash tree. She nudged at a still form lying next to her.

Don nestled the tiny lamb inside the front of his coveralls and started back to the barn. The mother sniffed for her baby, then followed. I am pretty sure Dad let her know his opinion of her intelligence as he locked her inside for the night.

Meanwhile Don hurried to the house with the baby that clung to life by barely a thread. Mom brought rags and they rubbed the small creature until the frozen clumps thawed and the gray, wooly coat was dry. The little guy hardly moved as they laid him on a thick towel in a cardboard box and placed it next to the warm cook stove. His side moved up and down feebly before we went to bed that night. Don rubbed the little black head and looked up at our mother. "I don't think he'll make it, but at least we tried."

The next morning Don woke with a start. What was that noise? He rushed to the kitchen to find a tipped-over box and a bleating baby fumbling around, pushing his nose into any opening he could find. Our brother was thrilled (Mom was relieved) as the newborn wobbled to his mother's side in the barn.

Spring rains and melting snow meant deep messes in the cow yard, and inevitably, at least one heifer (probably after researching the Birthing Pool) chose to deliver her first-born in the mud. During calving time, the guys took turns getting up at 2:00 AM to check for calves or cows having problems. One cold April morning Delmer stalked through the bovine obstetrics unit. Next to a feeder he saw a cow sniffing something on the ground. A closer look revealed a mud-coated creature flailing about, unable to stand in the slippery mire.

With an uncertain moo, the cow followed my brother as he dragged her calf out of the puddle. Then he ran back to the barn for the heavy plastic sled. The thick muck sucked at his overshoes as he wallowed through the barnyard, pulling the sled with the mud-coated baby lying on its side. In the dry barn, the mother watched warily as he rubbed her calf with rough gunny sacks, finally revealing dark brown fur. The cow took over from there and began bathing her unsteady offspring.

Some of the rescues did not involve livestock, but various wild critters that wandered about the Midwest prairies. I remember the look of regret in my dad's eyes when he carefully handed me his farmer cap, piled full of greenish-brown eggs. "I must have hit the mother duck with the sickle mower. Maybe one of the banties can hatch them?" He cautioned that they might not hatch, but we could sure try. Banties were born to be mothers, and sure enough one wanted to set. Less than a month later, the little mother hen stared in wonder at her four babies' webbed feet, but she loved them just the same.

In Laura Ingalls Wilder's The Long Winter, Pa found the wild cattle with heads frozen to the ground. My sister Deloris recalls from the Nooks and Crannies of her mind a similarly unusual incident when she was little. Dad called for help as he lumbered in the porch, lugging two bulging canvas bags. Deloris thought she saw the bags move as she followed him down the basement steps. He bent to open a sack. "They might not live," he warned his little girl, "but we have to try."

He brought out a light brown hen pheasant. Her head was coated in white ice with only a tiny breathing hole above the beak. She stood there, confused and blinded. Gently Dad and Deloris removed the frozen covering. Soon eleven wild birds, heads thawed, wandered about the cement floor. Within an hour, father and daughter carried the pheasants out near the haystack and released them after spreading a bucket of cracked corn on the ground.

Not all of the animal rescue operations had happy endings. Eggs did not always hatch. Some lambs and calves were lost in extreme harsh conditions. We all knew the risk. We knew that sometimes the creatures would die no matter how hard we worked to save them. We knew our hearts would hurt with the loss, but still, we had to try.

☼

So Much More than Just a Birthday

Excitement was in the air! I could feel it. My birthday was Wednesday, but Mom said that everyone was coming to celebrate on Sunday. One more day; I couldn't wait!

She wiped down the white metal cupboards in the kitchen, then sprinkled the porcelain sink with Old Dutch cleanser. "Can I help?" I asked. She handed me the dust rag from under the sink, and I headed for the living room. Normally, when I dusted I "hit the high spots," but since it was for my birthday, I did a better job. I even moved the ceramic kitties off their doily and dusted under them. I was still working when Mom brought in the spray can of Pledge and her own rag. Guess she knew my work history. "I'll just get the places you can't reach." She smiled as she worked, and five minutes later lemon clouds hovered over the piano and bookcase.

Once the house was spiffy, Mother stirred up the cake. I requested white with cooked brown sugar icing. As she worked she recited the menu for the next afternoon. Ham salad on homemade buns. Open-face Cheez Whiz on rye bread with olive slices on top. Jell-O with fruit cocktail. Glorified rice. Pickles. I felt pretty special, imagining a whole table of good food prepared just for my birthday.

At last Sunday afternoon arrived. Mom let me wear my pink print Easter dress, but only under the condition that I "take good care of it." Visions of a royal birthday princess danced in my head. How could anything happen to my dress while I sat primly at the table, surrounded by my noble court?

An aunt and uncle and two of their boys arrived just after 2:00. The boys peeked in the door. Instantly, my brother and older sisters rounded up the bat, ball and gloves and followed the boys back outside. Uncle Oscar walked in, greeted Dad and they strolled to the living room. Soon a farmer discussion of the need for rain and the price of corn drifted from the next room. Mom greeted Ida warmly. Then Ida leaned on the counter next to Mom, who swished soapy water over the last dishes. Laughter quickly followed as the two chatted away happily.

Mom changed into a clean apron, a purple gingham embellished with cross stitching along the bottom and pocket. At last, Aunt Ida turned away from the counter and spotted me sitting all alone. "Oh, I almost forgot. Happy birthday, DeAnn."

Just then another vehicle rumbled into the driveway. Aunt Julia and Grandma soon joined us. Mom and Ida swooped in to greet them and quickly all the women gathered around the table, sharing events that had happened since their last visit, my uncle's birthday two months earlier.

I sat at the corner of the table, feeling a bit left out. Julia must have noticed; she motioned for me to move my chair right next to her and rested her hand on my shoulder. "Things were different back when I was seven,"

she smiled wistfully and the conversation turned to my aunts' growing-up memories. I became engrossed with their stories and the afternoon flew by.

Mom and her sisters had similar-sounding laughs---giggles, actually. Julia recounted a story of an angry goose that chased Uncle Elmer through the yard and right up the porch steps. He quickly grabbed a broom to protect himself. The women got to laughing so hard at the image of their brother wielding a broom that their shoulders shook and tears streamed down their cheeks.

Still recovering from the giggle marathon, Grandma and the aunts worked together to get lunch on the table. Upon hearing the word "food," the ball players hurried in, gulped down a glass of Kool Aid, grabbed a sandwich in each hand and headed back out for one more game. The adults filled plates and returned to favorite spots.

After enjoying two refills of coffee cups and slices of moist, caramel-topped cake, Grandma found her purse and produced a card with my name on it. Julia and Ida each set a small package in front of me. "Happy Birthday!"

For a time I had been so absorbed in the stories and laughter I had forgotten. I thanked each of them as I opened their gifts. A crisp dollar bill, a Little Golden Book, The Pokey Little Puppy, and a child-size handkerchief, edged with a delicate turquoise lace Julia had crocheted.

All too soon, the guests gathered their belongings and said their goodbyes. Aunt Julia called back as she opened the porch door. "Next month at my house."

"I'll bring the birthday cake," Mom announced, already smiling in anticipation.

I won't claim to any philosophical enlightenments at the age of seven about family gatherings. At that time I never thought about life on the farm. How families worked hard, stayed home and sometimes went for weeks without seeing anyone else. It has taken me fifty-some years and a dreadful pandemic to come to the profound realization. A birthday was a reason to get together. To laugh and remember. To share treasured time with loved ones.

It was about so much more than just a birthday.

Learn by Doing Among Other Things

I ripped open the envelope and pulled out the piece of paper. It was a check. I stared at the numbers for a few seconds, and soon the wheels in my head, treaded with dollar signs, began turning. We received money for every ribbon we won at Achievement Days, our Kingsbury County Fair in De Smet, South Dakota. If I earned almost seven dollars with ribbons I won this year (making only one or two tiny mistakes), just think of the money I could rake in if I took more stuff. Why, that 4-H premium check could be a major source of income!

I looked back at my first year in 4-H. Since my five older siblings had excelled every year, it was expected that I keep up the tradition. At the spring planning meeting Mother and the "Little Sisters" club leader, Mrs. Russell, had helped me decide what to exhibit. Girls were expected to sew something (my sisters had made skirts, blouses and dresses), so "cotton table cloth" and "apron" appeared on my list. I wrinkled my nose, but figured I had plenty of time to whip them up--later. Those lazy, hazy, crazy days of summer slipped by and finally Mom said it was time. She sat next to me, continually encouraging. A length of adhesive tape an inch from the needle made a track to follow. I pushed my leg next to the "go" lever and the needle flew up and down. I managed to sew all the way around the green checkered square. Then Mother showed me how to pull out the strings on each side to make a frayed edge around the tablecloth.

We cut the pieces for the apron out of blue and white gingham. Mom taught me how to gather the top of the skirt by sewing it first with a long stitch. I broke the gathering thread at least three times and had to tear it out and start over. Frustrated, I tossed the garment down, ready to quit. Never losing patience, our mother assured me that that is how we learn—from our mistakes. Then she got out her seam ripper for me. Finally, the apron was about done. I pressed the hem and pinned it, only poking my fingers ten times or so. The machine zipped along. All at once I ran off the edge of the hem for a few stitches. A quick glance at Mom told me she hadn't seen it, so I steered back on the hem and kept going. Why didn't I stop? The whole seam had to be taken out. I hated that seam ripper!

The day before fair Delmer helped me pick five nice onions and carrots out of the piles that we dug from the garden. I brushed the dirt off the dry brown onion skins, scrubbed and trimmed the carrots, and arranged them on a paper plate.

Exhibit Day dawned. Mom instructed me to mix up my oatmeal cookies while she helped Delmer get his chickens ready. I wanted to watch them wipe down the white feathers and rub olive oil on the feet and combs, but I had to stay in the kitchen. Having practiced several times, I knew the recipe by heart. I got out the ingredients and blended the margarine and sugar. Soon it was all mixed, and I dropped spoons full of dough onto cookie sheets. Mother hurried in just in time to help bake them.

As we searched for five uniform cookies, she noticed that these looked different from my other batches. "Did you remember the oatmeal?"

There was barely enough time to make a new batch.

Two months later, gazing at the check for exhibit premiums, my get-rich-quick scheme chased away all memories of my mistakes. I dreamed of what I would take to the fair next year. Delmer and Don always got purple ribbons on their Duroc hogs. All you had to do was follow your pig around in the ring and look at the judge once in a while. How difficult was that? Maybe Dad would let me take one.

Deloris had scored highest in poultry judging when she was a junior, winning a trip to Chicago. She could give me pointers and I could exhibit chickens and eggs.

Deloris, Darlene and Dorothy had won purples on their demonstrations. They had made milk drinks and deviled eggs with cottage cheese and un-baked chocolate cookies. It all looked easy to me.

So, the next spring at our club's planning meeting I was ready. Mrs. Russell handed out papers for us to list what we wanted to exhibit. "Learn by Doing" the 4-H slogan, was centered at the top. An excellent leader, she encouraged us to try new projects as well as improve on last year's.

Mom sat next to me as I compiled my list. Pig. Chickens. Eggs. Onions, carrots, green beans and potatoes. Dairy foods demonstration. Poster on oatmeal cookies. Mom's lips turned up just a little. Banana bread. Mother glanced up at Mrs. Russell. They were probably wondering what banana bread would be like without the bananas.

I watched all the other club members intently adding to their lists. At last I penciled in my final item, "cotton dress." I did not notice then, but I am pretty sure our mother tensed at the image, then looked up, silently seeking help from Above.

Resisting the urge to chew on the eraser, I thought carefully. I shook my head. Finally, I scratched three dark lines through that last item and plopped down the pencil.

Mom breathed a huge sigh of relief. She remembered the seam ripper, too.

Eat It; It's Good for You!

A spoon full a day keeps the doctor away. Our parents took a preventative approach to child health care, which included a daily dose of cod liver oil for Deloris and Donald. "It's good for you," Dad maintained as he expectantly held out the spoon. They opened their mouths and swallowed the gross, disgusting, smelly, oily liquid. Too bad Mary Poppins had not been created then. A spoonful of sugar definitely would have helped the medicine go down!

One advantage of being farther down in the birth order—the folks lightened up a bit on the health regimen. The last four kids only had to take cod liver oil when we didn't feel well, which was bad enough.

Researching the benefits of the fish oil, I discovered that scientists believe it can help support eye health, reduce the risk of heart disease, improve digestion, ward off anxiety and fight inflammation. Mom and Dad didn't have Google. They did not spend a lot of time conferring with health professionals, but as was often the case, people in their generation were ahead of their time in their life philosophies.

As my siblings and I searched back into the nooks and crannies of our minds, every one of us started with the same statement. "We didn't get sick very often." Possibly it was all the fresh clean South Dakota air we enjoyed during the many hours we played outside. Or the homegrown vegetables and fruits we helped raise and preserve. Mom made a salad with the first lettuce using a vinegar and cream dressing. Green beans, carrots (they're good for your eyes) and cabbage appeared on our table all winter long. Whether we liked them or not, we were expected to try a few bites. "Eat it; it's good for you."

The latest foodie fad: fermentation. Mother did not know that her sauerkraut, beet pickles, bean pickles and dill pickles provided probiotics that strengthened her family's immune systems. She just figured pickling provided a fast, easy method to preserve food.

No, we were not sick very often as we grew up. Delmer remembers spending a few days in a dark bedroom when he caught measles and chicken pox.

A "stomach bug" kept someone home from a day of school on rare occasions. When we finally felt well enough to venture out of bed, Mom would cautiously guide us as to when and how much liquid we should take.

Once in a while one of us got off the school bus not feeling well. Mom seriously studied our eyes and told us to go lie down on the davenport. Later, after chores, Dad would kneel down next to us and gently rest his big work-worn hand on our forehead. (He and Mom possessed built-in thermometers.) Then he quietly told us to feel better, and we always did.

Sometimes a bad cold settled in and Mom administered her time-worn remedy. She applied a generous coating of Vicks VapoRub to our neck and chest and back. Then she draped a length of heavy wool around our neck and pinned it at the shoulder. The Vicks and wool warmed us and cleared congestion. The itchy fabric rubbing on the neck with every move speedily stifled sniffles.

Later, to hasten healing, we sat down to a supper of chicken soup with homemade noodles or with fluffy dumplings floating on top. Sometimes Mother made her special comfort food, custard. The baked dessert of milk and eggs, sprinkled with nutmeg was the ultimate easy-on-the-tummy food.

We always felt loved and cared-for, but it seemed to me the folks tried pretty hard not to give us too much attention when we were sick. No sense encouraging it after all. Delmer remembers waking up one spring morning with the brilliant idea that he might get out of going to school for a day if he pleaded sick. Mom felt his forehead. Dad felt his forehead. Dad told Delmer to get up and come to the kitchen. Dad poured some cod liver oil into a spoon. "Here, take this; it will help you feel better." Delmer got a whiff of the disgusting smell and wrinkled his nose. Dad persisted, "Eat it; it's good for you."

Delmer never tried playing sick again. How's that for preventative medicine?

MOM'S COMFORT CUSTARD

2 cups milk
2 eggs
½ cup sugar
½ teaspoon vanilla
1 Tablespoon butter
nutmeg
Grapenuts

In a small saucepan, heat milk to just under the boiling point. Let cool slightly.

In a large bowl, beat eggs, sugar and vanilla. Add warmed milk and mix well. Pour mixture into custard cups. Drizzle a small amount of butter over each cup. Add a teaspoon of Grapenuts and sprinkle with nutmeg.

Place the filled custard cups in a pan of water. (I use a 9 x 13 cake pan with an inch of water on the bottom.) Carefully place the pan in a preheated 350 degree oven. Bake until custard top is golden brown, 35 to 40 minutes.

Deep Dishwater Discussions

"We need a dishwasher," I sighed as I reluctantly stacked the plates on the table and carried them to the counter, plopping them down with a bit more force than necessary. I knew there was no hope of getting a dishwasher; Mom had her own way of doing things. But I pleaded my case just the same. Hearing the clatter of dishes, she glanced over with a frown, then placed a bowl of leftover potatoes into the fridge. With both hands I gathered the pile of silverware the four of us had used for supper and dropped them recklessly next to the plates.

Having raised five kids before me, Mother knew when something was bothering us. "How was school today?" she finally asked, probably hoping I would start talking before I grabbed the really breakable stuff.

"Horrible," I replied. "We did not get to play ball, not even during noon hour." Mom hurried to snatch up her fragile glasses.

Dad and Mom's wedding photo.

"Somebody shot a spit wad when the teacher was writing on the chalkboard. It whizzed right next to her ear. There it stuck. Smack on the old blackboard! By the time she turned around we were all staring down at our desks. She asked who shot the spit wad. Nobody would confess, so we all had to stay in every recess. How come we all had to be punished because of one dumb kid? He should have known not to shoot it when she was standing right there. It's just not fair."

I had calmed down a bit as I reached into the drawer for a clean dish towel. An adorable kitten embroidered on the front of the towel sat next to a scrub board. "Monday Wash" was neatly stitched under the cat. The sharply-pressed folds stood out on the pristine white cloth as I shook it open. "How about if we just let the dishes dry in the drainer? Think of all the work it would save."

That got a rise out of Mother as she hauled the Dutch oven from the stove. She had her own way of doing things. "I don't want my glasses looking like the dog licked them." Since I loved the dog I didn't think that would be so terrible.

Mom squeezed a generous squirt of Dove for Dishes into the dishpan and turned on the hot water faucet. The subtle scent of lily of the valley wafted into the air as Mom carefully placed the wheat-printed glasses into the water. Having released my anger into words, frustration dissipated like the steamy vapor. I gently pushed the towel into the first glass. "What was it like when you went to school, Mom?"

Her hands swished through the sparkling suds for a few seconds. "There were times when I thought things were unfair, too. I was left-handed. Back then the teacher thought everyone should write with their right hand. She got out her ruler and if I reached for the slate pencil with my left hand, it got smacked."

Somehow missing recess seemed pretty trivial after that. Though I did not realize it then, those talks as Mom washed and I dried proved far more valuable than labor saving devices. From the nooks and crannies of my mother's mind poured precious memories.

She grew up during the Depression. She and her sisters carried a lunch pail to school. Sometimes lunch consisted of a slice of bread spread with lard or some other kind of fat.

The girls in the family had to quit school after graduating eighth grade. They were needed to work at home. Mom and her sisters sometimes milked up to thirty Holsteins by hand. When she was sixteen, Mom walked to a neighbor's to help with housekeeping and childcare. They paid her seventy-five cents a week.

She and her sister Ida were confirmed together. Before confirmation they had to recite for the preacher. They were good at memorizing, since country school required much of that. Our mother could rip off "The Gettysburg Address," "Paul Revere's Ride" and the entire roster of U.S. presidents without a miss. Reciting the Small Catechism was a piece of cake.

As I dried and stacked slightly-chipped dime store plates, evenings flitted away in our South Dakota kitchen, and family history passed on to one more generation. My grandpa died before I was born, but I grew to know him from Mom's stories. Two of her brothers went to war. One fought at Normandy. Neither talked about the battles.

When Mom and Dad first got married, their only furniture was peach crates, stacked on end. From sunup to sundown she worked next to him in the fields. Her life had not been easy, but she neither whined nor complained. Like sloshing soapy water over a soup bowl, she did what needed to be done.

Mom was not always the one standing in front of our kitchen sink. When my sisters got old enough, it was their job to do the supper dishes. Usually, the oldest washed and the younger girls dried. Certain that there was more to life than doing dishes, they hurried through the task.

As the youngest I was the lucky one. With a dishtowel in hand and the scent of Dove dish soap lingering in the air I learned about old times and family and life. I learned to say what was on my mind, then put it in perspective. I learned to listen.

Looking back, I am glad Mom never heeded my pleas for a dishwasher. To this day I am very thankful that our mother had her own way of doing things.

☀

What's a Picture Really Worth?

"A picture is worth a thousand words." The phrase came into use in the early part of the 20th century. At that time the words commended the effectiveness of graphics in advertising. It is believed the phrase was adapted from a Chinese proverb: One picture is worth ten thousand words.

Whether a thousand or ten thousand, the word value of the three huge tubs of photos stacked before us was equivalent to a mountain of dictionaries. Our mother had accumulated countless pictures throughout her 96 years of life. She labeled and sorted and gave away, but many remained. Though we all enjoyed a photo journey through the old days, the massive task loomed over my siblings and me on this day of our annual family reunion: to sort and divide thousands of printed images.

Deloris got us going as we lounged around her dining room table. We lugged the first case to a chair and opened the top envelope. Out fell a menagerie of very old formal photographs. Dark pressed-board background framed thick prints. Gray marbled folders begged to be opened. The work of professional photographers, their embossed or gilded insignia adorned the bottom: McKibben of De Smet, and A. Swancutt of Bryant, S.D. The subjects stood or sat stiffly, faces molded in a serious pose. No smiles back then. In wedding photographs, often the man sat. His new bride posed at his side in her wedding finery. As we read Mom's notes on the back and passed the pictures around the table, we joked that their facial expressions reflected second thoughts on their new state of matrimonial bliss.

Uncle Elmer, who served in WWII.

The next layer was manila envelopes stuffed with small, glossy black and white prints sporting scalloped edges. From the nooks and crannies of our minds emerged an image of our father, head bent over a black "box" as he centered us in the view finder and pushed the button. The black box was a Brownie, one in a series of simple and inexpensive cameras made by Eastman Kodak. Dad loaded the film and cranked the lever on the side to advance it for each picture. The roll of exposed film was mailed in to be developed into photos. The total cost of film and developing ran under two dollars. Since you paid for every picture (faces, feet or sky!) a lot of time was spent placing the tall people in the back and making sure everybody's face showed, hopefully with eyes open.

In contrast to the old professional photos, these displayed smiling faces even though "Say Cheese" had not yet been coined. Kids sitting in a wagon or on a sled. Adults in front of a car. When we had visitors, Dad got out the camera and we lined up for a picture.

As each precious print circled the table, memories surfaced. Sometimes we had to stop for a story. The faded brown paper crackled as we opened another package. This one was heavier, and immediately we saw color.

Technology fascinated our father. Teaching his children how things worked was as important to him as preserving history with photos. Shortly after Polaroid cameras were introduced, the whole family discovered how a print developed as we gathered around Dad and his new camera.

He snapped the picture, waited a few seconds, pulled out the perforated paper, then peeled off the filmy tissue. A distinctive odor permeated the air as we watched the last details form. Those glossy Polaroid prints reminded us of opening Christmas presents and blowing out birthday candles.

Lilly, Julia and Ida's confirmation photo. (Mom's sisters)

Rose Hill School #12 Halloween Party. (Deloris Gilbertson)

The piles at the end of the table grew as we chose a new home for each photograph. The level remaining in the first tub dwindled. One memory stirred up another. Deloris' cookies disappeared. The coffeepot brewed record refills.

Silent prayers of thanks rose when we announced the last packages which were loaded with square white-bordered prints. We recalled that Dad replaced the Polaroid with a Kodak. Flash bulbs or flash cubes allowed inside pictures. A cube was supposed to provide four flashes. Occasionally, much to the photographer's frustration, one side didn't flash or we forgot to keep track of the flashes and snapped a photo when the cube was all used up. Occasionally we played Guess Who with a really dark print when the photos came in the mail.

Then Instamatics came out. Quantity and subject matter increased drastically as we all became photographers. The pictures proved it. Showing animals at the fair. Lincoln Memorial. Mom with her flowers. Dad's new car. Graduations. Confirmations. Baptisms. New grandchildren. Trips to see new grandchildren. The dog. My cat. My other cat.

Though the time had passed quickly in pleasant camaraderie, we released a collective sigh of relief as the last photo landed on its designated spot.

Each bagged up our haul, promised to make requested copies, and resolved to take on another batch next summer. We shook our heads as we stared at the remaining tubs, wondering how we ever thought we could get through them all in one day.

I jumped up. "Wait a minute! Everybody line up for a picture."

I grabbed my digital. Automatic flash. Automatic focus. Push a button to delete the bad ones. (Dad would have been impressed.) Caught up in the moment (and the relief of completing the picture-sorting task), I clicked close-ups and not-so-close-ups and every possible angle until at last "cheese" turned to "STOP!"

Sheesh. Didn't they know what those pictures were worth?

Me in front of the family car.

To Wrinkle-Free With Love

Wood clunked on wood as Mom angled into the door and rested the bulky panel on the floor. She sucked in a big breath, grasped both sides and lugged it into the kitchen. The white fabric-covered board pointed upward while she lowered the legs, then bent the arm and pushed it into the first slot of the wooden base. Grabbing the cushioned top, Mother set up her ironing board.

I laid my favorite doll, Susan, on a chair and ran to get my own board, a replica of Mom's. While I set mine up, Mother got out her iron and plugged it in. I watched her turn the dial on the top, then set the device up on its back. One more trip for the ironing basket, a wooden "apple" crate lined with green plastic that fit over the wire handles.

Yesterday, when we brought the clothes in from the line, Mom folded, sorted and put away. Everything that needed ironing (which seemed like most of the stash!) waited in the middle of the table to be sprinkled.

The sprinkler was a tall, glass bottle with a cork stopper that fit tightly. A metal dome-shaped cover nested in the center of the cork. Perforated with holes, the sprinkler resembled a salt shaker that dispensed water instead.

Mom let me sprinkle the hankies, dish towels and aprons. I flapped each item down on the Formica table top, tipped the bottle and attempted to distribute water droplets evenly over the fabric surface. Then I tucked in sides, rolled them into tight scrolls and placed them in the ironing basket, keeping similar things together. Mother sprinkled the shirts, dresses, aprons, pants and sheets, covered the basket and lugged it to the cool porch until the next day.

Tuesday morning we were ready! Mom licked the index finger of her right hand and lightly touched it to the bottom of the preheated iron. The tiny "pffft" indicated the Goldilocks standard on temperature—just right.

First the hankies, the pretty ones and the men's big white ones, then the big red or blue bandannas the guys kept in their work pockets. She flapped each open on the padded surface of her ironing board and rubbed the shiny flat base over it. Little "sizzles" puffed into steam as Mom ran the tip over wet spots in the corners.

Sometimes our mother would tell me about ironing when she grew up. The board was the same, but there were no electric irons. Several "sad irons" or heavy metal bases heated on the cook stove. The person doing the ironing attached a wooden handle to one of the hot irons and hurried to the board to smooth out wrinkles. When that one cooled off she had to replace it with a hot one from the stove. It was sweaty, hard work and difficult to assure the proper temperature of the iron. Too cool and stubborn wrinkles remained; too hot and the iron burned an ugly scorch mark that branded that item forever.

"It's a lot easier to iron now," she said as she grabbed a damp dish towel from the basket. It draped over the side of the board, so she ironed part of it, then pulled the towel up on the board and ran the hot device over the next section. When the wrinkles were all ironed out, Mother folded in one side, pressed it, then the other, until a neat square fairly sparkled in front of her, a sweet embroidered kitten centered perfectly on the front. I noticed a smile on Mom's face as she glided the iron quickly over it one more time. Piles of neatly folded wrinkle-free laundry grew on the table.

Meanwhile, a wonderful aroma filled the room. In the nooks and crannies of my mind, this fragrance rivaled that of fresh chocolate chip cookies. It was a comforting blend of fresh air and Tide. The whole house felt warm and cozy.

Though she folded the white cotton sheets in half, one corner touched the floor. Soon the big bundle flattened into neat layers. I glided my own iron, a maroon-colored ceramic model, over my doll blanket. I pushed the black handle down harder to smooth the wrinkles. "Bring it here," Mom said, her blue eyes sparkling. She ran her nifty appliance over it. Susan felt warm and cuddly wrapped in her sleek pink blanket.

It didn't seem long until Mother unplugged the iron and moved it to the cutting board to cool safely far back on the counter. She folded up the ironing board and put it away. Tuesday ironing was done.

At a recent visit with my dear 100-year-old friend, she happily recalled using a mangle-iron. Having no clue what a mangle was, I had to Go Google. I learned that the device ran hot rollers over the pieces of laundry making quick, efficient work of removing wrinkles. Sheets ran through in seconds. Pants displayed a perfect crease.

In my imagination I can hear Dad asking, "Mabel, do you want one of those fancy new ironing things with the rollers? It would mean a lot less time standing next to that ironing board."

Possibly she remembered how much more difficult ironing had been when she was young. Or she might have thought of the wonderful warm smells that enveloped her as she glided the iron over her loved ones' shirts and dresses. Maybe she knew there were no "toy" mangles, and she would miss her daughters' pretend-ironing next to her. Whatever her reasons, I am pretty sure she would have answered, "Nah, I don't need one of those things. I love to iron."

Because she did.

☀

Ready for Reading, Writing, and 'Rithmetic

A thunderstorm had swept through during the night, eliminating any chance of field work. The men made quick work of chores, and Mom fixed a hearty breakfast. Soon we all piled in our '57 Ford Fairlane. Darlene and Dorothy and the boys crowded into the back. I sat between Mom and Dad in the front. Dad at the wheel, we headed for Huron. Forty miles away, it offered an array of stores just right for school shopping.

The girls chattered excitedly in the back. I heard something about a dress and saddle shoes. Don and Delmer didn't say much. Probably, they would rather be home, fishing.

No new dresses for me today. One more year until I started first grade. Dad said the board discussed adding kindergarten to the classes at our school in Erwin, but I was happy that hadn't happened yet. What was so great about sitting in a stuffy desk all day? And you had to wear shoes, even when it was nice out! Then there was that huge scary bus that stopped out at the end of the driveway. Dad made it clear that the Wolkow kids had better be waiting when it came. I preferred watching from a distance.

Dorothy said school was fun. She liked being with her friends, and she told me I will learn a lot. I couldn't think of much I wanted to learn that I didn't already know. Before Deloris went to Northwest College of Commerce, she taught me how to sound out words. I could already read every one in the True Blue Contest Speller first grade list. I didn't mind staying home another year.

Dad pulled into a parking spot downtown close to Penney's. He took the boys to their section to find jeans, shirts and underclothing. I followed Mom and the girls. All at once I spotted a display of soft-looking skirts with poodles on them. Pink and gray and black wool made a soft background for the poufy-tailed white dogs that were stitched to the bottom front of the circles. Mom strode by them quickly. "They'll be out of style before long."

On rainy days she had helped my sisters sew skirts. Gathered at the waist, the pretty plaid fanned out over can-can slips. I thought they were prettier than the poodle skirts, mainly because I liked collies better. Mom must have thought so too. On a mission, she headed directly to the dresses. Hand-me-downs provided most of our family's back-to-school wardrobes, so the girls were thrilled to choose one new dress and a blouse.

It took a while to try on favorites and decide. Finally, with garments draped over arms, we wandered through the rest of the girls' section. Darlene smiled when Mother grabbed two thick packages of white bobby socks. We met the guys in the boys' department, made the purchases and headed up the street to the shoe store.

Later, Dorothy and Darlene verbally pictured their first-day-of-school wardrobe, obviously of critical importance, as we trekked to Woolworth's. Greeted at the door by an enticing aroma, my tummy growled loudly. Probably worried that she would lose me to the food counter, Mom grabbed my hand, and the entire family paraded back to the school supply aisles.

The high schoolers needed typing paper, notebook paper, and folders. Three-ring binders helped even those who preferred basketball to homework to be better organized. Dad picked up a pack of ten Bic pens. Mom said we had plenty of pencils at home.

Dorothy and Delmer needed colors. I saw Delmer gaze at the big box of 48 that opened up and displayed all those beautiful colors as though they stood on stair steps. Mom grabbed two boxes of 24. Delmer's face fell.

Finally, satisfied that they had provided everything necessary for their children to begin another year of school, our parents herded us back to the food counter. We each sat on a tall stool with a red vinyl seat that twirled in a circle. Mom frowned when I discovered the twirling part. Dad ordered seven hot beef sandwiches. In a few minutes the waitress, dressed in a white uniform and apron (and a hairnet that squished her curls flat) set the steaming plates in front of us. Rich dark-brown gravy flooded the mashed potatoes and slices of roast beef that rested on a slice of white bread. Relishing those mashed potatoes, I decided school shopping wasn't so bad even if I didn't get a new dress.

A month later, school was in full swing. One Monday night when the dishes were done, I watched as my siblings walked into the kitchen. One by one they carried books, paper, pens and pencils and pulled a chair up to the table. Donald read a huge book with tiny words and no pictures. Darlene, left-handed, wrote something in beautiful curvy writing. Dorothy read from a school book and scribed pretty loops, also with her left hand. Delmer scrawled big numbers on paper, drew lines under them, and then wrote more numbers under the line.

Feeling a bit left out, I pilfered a few sheets of Mom's paper stash (the backs of cards and envelopes that still had plenty of writing space) and pulled the cigar box of worn-down and naked colors from the phone cabinet. I crawled up on an empty chair. I picked out violet and proceeded to make rows and rows of squiggles on the paper. Under the squiggles I scribbled the numbers from one to 50. Looking over my work, I felt better knowing that I could do reading, writing and arithmetic. Just like my brothers and sisters.

But I was still glad I didn't have to go to school—yet.

Tough it Up and Carry On

Though there were others, a search through the nooks and crannies of my mind reveals only one incident that I can actually remember going to the doctor. Dad took me to the office. A nurse ushered me into a room where I was told to lie on my stomach on the table. Within seconds I felt a shooting pain in my backside. I jerked and voiced a rather loud "owww!" This resulted in no sympathy. No sucker or stickers. I was coldly instructed to get up and go back to the waiting room.

Mom and Dad occasionally related a story of my much-earlier experience in the doctor's office. When I was little, I had some sort of cyst on the back of my head that bled profusely with the slightest bump. When you are three, bumps happen quite often. The doctor prescribed cauterization. The first time went fine, according to my parents, but the cyst grew back. Months later, when the nurse wheeled the same cauterizing machine into the room, I narrowed my eyes, mustered up all the courage a little girl can muster and ordered, "You put that thing away!" Those words were probably the closest to whining we ever got. Of course, she ignored me. At least the bloody thing did not grow back again.

Dorothy needed to stay in the Huron hospital when the doctor removed a dark mole from her face. Only a third grader, tears fell when Dad went home and she had to spend the night all alone. Knowing that complaining would accomplish nothing, she toughed it through the night.

Delmer clearly recalls his stay in the hospital when he broke his arm. It happened during noon recess on a cold winter day in Erwin. A popular playground attraction, the tall pipe-framed swings beckoned to the older boys. A fourth grader, Delmer grabbed both ropes on the middle swing, pulled himself up on the two-by-six board, and proceeded to pump his legs rapidly back and forth. Soon, my brother proudly realized he was soaring higher than the boys on either side. An adrenaline rush pulsed through him as he scoped the ground below. A few yards ahead of the swings lay a soft white snow drift, gently sculpted by the South Dakota wind.

A glorious image of flying through the air flashed through the young boy's imagination. All at once, he "sort of fell." His flight scored an Olympic 2 instead of his envisioned 10. He crashed right through the snow drift, landing with a sickening crunch on his right arm. An older boy, Elwyn, helped him into the school. The superintendent took one look at the protruding bone, called the folks and went to get Dorothy to wait with her brother.

Dad drove him to the doctor in De Smet. For some reason, the waiting time extended through two hours as the boy endured excruciating pain. At last, the nurse escorted them to the exam room. The doctor walked in the door wielding a huge syringe with a three-inch needle. Dad remarked to his son later that he wondered if it would come out the other side of the arm. In spite of the ominous needle, the shot did not alleviate the pain.

After a few minutes, the doctor grasped Delmer's hand and elbow simultaneously and pulled. At once the pain subsided as though the bones had been set in place. Doc wrapped the arm in plaster gauze and then formed the cast with layer upon layer of off-white plaster. Finally, Delmer was ready to go home, but that was not to be.

Concerned that the wrist and hand would swell from the two broken bones, the doctor ordered a stay in the Huron hospital. Delmer recalls that night as one of the longest in his life.

A pungent odor of antiseptic hung in the air, stinging Delmer's nostrils with each breath. Every time he came close to dozing, the squeak of leather shoes on waxed linoleum echoed down the hall. The nurse, dressed in white from her stiffly starched cap to her practical white footwear, strode in and checked his wrist. She spoke no words of comfort or encouragement. Obviously, she did not want to know how he felt. Her bedside manner exuded the message, loud and clear: Tough it up! The telltale "Squeak, squeak" grated in his ears as she stepped out the door until the next time.

The following day Dad and Mom rescued Delmer from the hospital and stopped at the College of Commerce to pick up Deloris for the weekend. She crawled in the back seat. Tears filled her eyes when she saw the cumbersome cast on her little brother's arm. He hefted up the heavy, rigid mass and shot her his silly grin.

Through our growing-up years we survived breaks, bumps and bruises and the occasional visit to a doctor's office. We toughed it up. When we had to, we bravely (mostly) endured pain and carried on. No sense whining. No sense complaining. It wouldn't have made any difference.

Looking Through the Steering Wheel

On our farm in eastern South Dakota, we learned to drive at a very young age. The requirement: our feet had to reach the pedals. No need to see over the steering wheel; looking through it worked just fine.

Dad needed help with farming, so when Donald and Delmer were seven, each crawled up on the tractor seat with Dad for driving lessons. Eyes sparkling, the little boys turned the wheel and circled around the yard. Stopping was the hard part. Dad told them they had to be strong enough to pull back the clutch lever, which extended up from the floor of the machine. Determination prevailed. Soon they deftly maneuvered the John Deere through fields and pastures, pulling grain wagons, hay racks and the manure spreader.

Driving the pickup naturally followed driving tractor. The gray 1954 Ford hauled fence posts, pulled trailers, hunted stray calves, delivered lunch; the vehicle proved invaluable all around the farm. Of course, the clutch and brake pedals protruded from the floor. Short legs reached to the pedals and had to push the clutch down far enough to be able to shift gears.

Delmer remembers mastering the gear shift from first to second. Comfortable with putzing along, my brother managed to get where he needed to go. One warm spring day, barely able to see over the steering wheel, Delmer drove out of the oat field and headed for home. Dad sat in the back, balancing four bags of seed.

Possibly, Dad was in a hurry to get home. Possibly, he knew that Delmer avoided shifting up into third gear and wanted him to learn. Whatever the reason, he tapped on the back window and ordered, "Shift up."

Traffic seldom posed a problem on our gravel road, but the ditches loomed steep, especially where spring rains washed away the sod. Nervous that he might miss third, Delmer focused intently on shifting. He pushed down the clutch with his left foot and stared down at the gearshift. He lifted it out of second, then eased it over and was about to shove it up into third when he looked up. The vehicle had swerved off the road. He slammed on the brakes just in time. Another foot and the pickup would have plunged off the edge of the huge cement culvert and into the crick.

Often, school events occurred when the folks were busy. At one time or another, we each had to get to Erwin, five miles away, for school activities. Deloris struggled to get the clutch down far enough to shift with her short legs. A dent in the mailbox and a scratch on the car door provided evidence of new-driver lessons.

Dorothy recalls having baton twirling practice at the school when Mom and Dad were unloading corn. Dad tossed her the keys to the pickup. "Keep it between the ditches." The girl's legs trembled, but she remembered watching Darlene when she learned to drive and powered through.

Our small country church snuggled between farm fields just a few miles north. Wednesday evening I had confirmation class. Dad pointed to the pickup. "You need to learn to drive a clutch first; then you can drive an automatic." He got in the passenger seat, proceeded to give me five minutes of lessons and sent me off. I did not look up at him when I killed the engine

West Bethany Lutheran Church in its new location near De Smet. (Dorothy Holter)

the first three times. At last the pickup lurched out to the road as I peered through the wheel.

Sweating bullets, I managed to get to the church. The other kids were sitting outside on the steps as I drove up. Their jaws dropped when they saw me drive up alone. I felt pretty cocky as I slid out and shut the pickup door.

When they enviously inquired about my driving, I just shrugged as though I did it all the time.

In an hour, class ended and again everyone piled out to the railings on the front steps. The pastor had assured us during class that we could talk to God about anything. I am pretty sure I prayed my way out of that church yard with all those eyes upon me. "Please, don't let me kill the engine. Please, don't let it jerk." It worked and I drove off into the sunset.

My siblings and I remember our mother smiling as she told a story about Don when he was barely four. He walked into her kitchen and announced that he was running away from home. Taken aback for a minute, the woman at last dried her hands on her apron and replied, "Well, when you run away you need clothes." She tied a clean shirt and underwear into a big red handkerchief. They found a long stick and attached the bundle to the end. "And you might get hungry." She slathered peanut butter onto a slice of bread and folded it in half.

With sandwich in hand and stick slung over his shoulder, Don headed out the front door. Mom watched as her little boy somberly walked out the gate and strode to the John Deere Model A tractor in the yard. He crawled up on the hard seat, leaned the stick on the tire and ate his sandwich. After a while he grasped the steering wheel with both hands, peered through, and turned it back and forth. For a long time Donald "drove" that tractor as though he had been driving for years. Finally, when an hour had passed, he scrambled down and trudged back into the kitchen. He set the clothes on the table and went back outside.

Yes, on the farm we learned to drive at a very young age.

Miracle in Our Midst

There was, and still is, something wonderful about having a new baby in the house. Different sounds, smells and textures surround us. All at once, the air nearly sparkles with excitement, though it must be subdued. (Don't wake the baby!) A sense of miracle whirls around even the youngest sibling, manifesting itself in total and compete wonder.

Deloris was not quite two when Don was born. I can imagine her pure delight as she climbed up on a chair to watch Mom lovingly dress the new baby. Her brother's head turned slowly and his dark, barely-focusing eyes found hers. She pressed a finger in his soft, warm palm and his tiny fingers closed around it, instantly forming a bond that lasted a lifetime.

Fourteen years elapsed between the births of the first and sixth child in our family. Now, it seems like years fly like the wind, but even during that time, things changed.

Back then, expecting a baby seemed more of a private thing. I am sure other adults knew, but the kids had to figure things out on their own. Dorothy recalls watching Mom standing at the kitchen table, cutting large white squares of fabric. Darlene, two years older and much wiser, informed her sister that Mom was going to have another baby.

The first four were born at home. The doctor made house calls. From the nooks and crannies of my mind I gather memories of Mom saying that women "used to have to stay in bed ten days when they had a baby." Maybe that's why our mother chose to stay home for the first four. She didn't have to follow hospital rules!

Delmer and I were born at De Smet Memorial Health Hospital. Mom didn't stay ten days, but she did stay

My mom and me.

more than the one or two days now required. Dr. Burman delivered me and Nurse Coughlin assisted.

At home all six of us slept in a wicker buggy for daytime naps; we were within hearing distance of Mom working in the kitchen. Some babies in those days slept in a bassinet until they were big enough for a crib.

Even terminology differed over the years. We never had a stroller, which were called prams, short for perambulators. When baby reached a few months of age, Pablum, or cereal, was added to his or her menu.

Speaking of "p" words, cloth diapers billowed in the wind on the clothes-line when babies lived at our house. Mother sewed them of outing flannel, a soft, warm, dense fabric with a twill weave that sported a nap on both sides. The diapers had to be fastened with huge diaper pins. Mom held her finger inside so she would not poke the baby. As she changed a diaper and pulled on rubber pants to prevent soaking through, she sometimes spoke of back when she cared for her baby brothers. "They didn't have rubber pants then. Just had soakers." Soakers were thick knitted pants that provided more layers. No disposable diapers, at least not at our house. I can't help but smile as I imagine Mom's opinion of such newfangled notions.

Babies wore sleepers that tied shut under the feet or "kimonos," long soft jackets that were open at the bottom and snapped closed down the front. Deloris, Darlene and Dorothy recall Mom swaddling the babies, wrapping them tightly in a homemade soft flannel receiving blanket. Years later, when the folks came to visit our new babies, I remember Mom helping. She smiled as she tucked in the ends of the little one's blanket so only her face peeked out. Then she said as she snuggled the baby on her shoulder, "They like to have their noses warm."

The most memorable blessed event ever (Okay, it was only memorable because all three of my sisters were old enough to remember.) was the birth of the youngest. They remember it "like yesterday." Dorothy got off the bus and raced to the house. There I was, lying on the davenport, sleeping like an angel. (She did comment that the angelic part occurred ONLY when I was sleeping.) Later, Dorothy watched as Mom lovingly bathed me at the same kitchen table where she cut out the diapers. She smiled and hummed the whole time.

Weeks later, Dorothy again watched Mom's tender-loving baby care. The little one smiled and kicked and moved her arms. Mom said, "She wants to be picked up." Dorothy did. That little baby snuggled her head into her sister's neck, which, (another miracle) fit just right.

Times have changed to be sure, but one thing remains certain; there is something wonderful about having a new baby in the house.

Chicken Soup—Or Not

I have a mean rooster.

From the Nooks and Crannies of my mind hatches a memory of the summer I lived in fear, fear of a rooster. It all began one evening when Mom sent me to the barn to look for eggs. A small flock of bantams lived in our barn, and the little hens took it as a challenge to hide their nests in the most unlikely places.

In summer much of the barn stood empty as the calves and sheep cavorted in the sunshine; this provided more secret hideaways. The distinctive smells of hay and livestock greeted me as I entered the aisle between the pens. I checked the obvious spots, the manger in the sheep pen and the feed troughs in front of the stanchions. No eggs. Heading back to the open door, I spotted a small opening under a shelf next to the straw pile. I peeked in, hoping to spot a light-colored oval, but I saw only darkness. I reached in slowly, thinking I would search by patting around. Lo and behold, my hand touched something soft—with feathers! Upset that I had discovered her secret, a little black hen flew out of that nest and cackled like the barn was on fire.

I reached back into the warm straw and found two smooth, light-brown eggs. I grabbed one in each hand and happily skipped toward the house. All at once I heard a noise, a pattering through the gravel. Something was coming up behind me--fast. I swerved around to find myself face to face with the banty rooster. He stopped abruptly and glared at me with angry, beady eyes.

Brooster

When you are six and not very tall, even a bantam rooster looks huge and scary. I didn't waste time trying to reason with him. I turned and ran. He was right behind me as I opened the gate and slammed it shut, right in his sharp-beaked face.

For several weeks after that, I avoided the barn. Every couple days Mom went with me to search for eggs. Finally, she said we would leave them in the nest. A few weeks later the little hen emerged from the barn with seven fluffy chicks. The rooster stayed close to his family, never tormenting me again.

Remembering that summer of terror, I swore I would not, under any conditions, ever allow a mean rooster in my flock. But last summer, eight adorable chicks pecked their way out of the eggs in my incubator. They grew up. Against my better judgment I decided to keep one rooster, the runt of the batch. He crowed incessantly, followed the hens around and avoided me. Several times I informed him that if he got mean, even once, he would become chicken soup. All was well until a few weeks ago.

Almost a year old, Brooster's spurs flashed in the sun as he strutted around the yard with his harem. He cackled a warning whenever I came to the coops, but I didn't pay much attention, until one day I was carrying a big yellow bucket into the chicken yard and something crashed into it from behind. I spun around to find Brooster, glaring at me with small, beady eyes. Thinking Chicken Noodle sounded good at the moment, I went after that rooster, the yellow bucket as my weapon. He challenged it once with his spurry, yellow feet and then ran. Feeling much braver at that point, and thankful that my neighbors are not within hearing distance, I yelled, "Come back and fight like a man!"

What to do with Brooster? I do not want to live in fear, but somehow chicken soup does not sound very appetizing. There must be another approach, but what?

Google has answers for everything. A rooster protects his flock. He is the alpha male. Show him who's boss. Don't challenge him. Look him in the eye. Never look him in the eye.

After another bucket attack, I decided that Brooster and I needed to have a little talk. At night all the chickens in the coop line up on their roost. Brooster was always right in front when I opened the side door. I reached in, grabbed him by the feet and carried him, (upside down because I wanted to show him who was boss) to my chicken-watching chair. He squawked like I was going through with the chicken soup threat.

Holding his legs very tightly, I held him up to look him in the eyes, well, eye. His comb flaps over one side covering the left eye like a pirate, so I turned his head to look him in the other eye. The glare flashed to something else. I hoped it was fear. He stopped his ruckus. Finally, I laid him on my lap and petted him. At first not too gently, but finally brushing my hands softly over his comb and head. I told him he couldn't be mean; after all, who feeds him and his flock?

The little pirate has not attacked since our heart-to-heart, but don't think I am not watching my back. Now, when I open the coop door at night, all the hens are lined up on the front roost. Brooster sits far back, out of reach.

I haven't mentioned anything about chicken soup again.

Something to Celebrate

An unusual silence hovered over us as we sat at the supper table that night in early May. A warm breeze drifted into the kitchen window, a reminder of the heat of the past week. Heat and wind that brought no rain. Old Man Winter had grudgingly bestowed mere inches of snow to renew the South Dakota prairies. With a farmer's never-waning faith, Dad and his sons had planted the oats, barley and wheat into dry dirt. Each passing day lessened the chances that the grain would sprout and grow. Would they need to replant? Should they even bother to plant the corn?

Mom and Dad grew up during the Thirties. For years, not enough rain or snow fell to sustain crops. Clouds of dust blackened the sky each day. Farms were lost. Children went hungry. The folks often spoke of the hard times during the drought. In the nooks and crannies of my mind a story lies waiting. Dad told of when he and his father loaded up the tin pails of honey their bees had produced and pedaled it around the country. A gallon of honey sold for a quarter. Though few families could afford even that, Grandpa managed to get a few dollars.

The rains had come again, and farming prospered over the last few years. Though memories of the past lurked in the back of our parents' minds, they did not speak of those bleak times that night at supper. Dad sat shirtless in his bib overalls, only one strap hooked. White shoulders and upper-arms contrasted with the dark tan below his elbows.

The meatloaf and mashed potatoes circled around. There would be leftovers tonight; no one was hungry. Mom tried to lighten the foreboding mood, asking the girls about the prom. Were their friends going? After short answers, quiet returned. Forks clicked on plates. Water glasses thumped lightly on the table.

Suddenly, something flashed through the windows. Dad glanced up for only a second. "Probably heat lightning." We cleaned our plates and waited for Mom to bring dessert, a bowl of home-canned applesauce. A gentle roll of thunder rumbled in the west.

We glanced at each other and held our breath. Could this mean rain? Dad kept his head down, refusing to allow hope to grow that would only die in dry dirt. Several times in the last week a storm cloud had rushed in. Thunder crashed. Lightning streaked the sky. Then twenty huge drops of rain plopped to the ground, puffing tiny clouds of dust that settled down next to miniature craters. Though Mom always tried to be positive, "Every drop helps," the few plops of moisture evaporated as quickly as they had come. Likely this would do the same.

A much cooler breath of air fluttered the lace curtains, ushering in the fresh, distinctive scent of rain. Thunder boomed, this time directly above. Dad's eyes met Mom's and he pushed his chair back. As he stepped out the front door onto the wooden stoop, the downpour began. We all piled out next to him. Soon bare feet danced through the grass, splashing as puddles formed. Rain washed over our faces and we looked up and tasted heaven. Mother stood behind Dad, beaming her smile through glistening eyes. Water replenished the earth.

Laughing, we finally wiped our feet on the thick porch rug and bounced into the kitchen. Still soaked, we sat back at the table and listened as the rain continued, like a happy song on the roof. We chattered merrily as we dished our bowls of applesauce.

Dad ran his hand over the top of his smooth head, wiping off pearls of rain. Chuckling, he looked around at his brood as water dripped from our hair. His eyes landed on Don and Delmer. "As soon as it dries off, maybe next week, we'll get the corn planted." The boys nodded a smile, then reached for one of Mom's molasses cookies.

The following essay was published only in the *Missouri Valley Times-News.* It is my heartfelt tribute to a dear woman. Billie's support and encouragement is one reason I keep writing. Thank you, Billie!

"I can't wait!"
Reflections on a Life Truly Lived

A Tribute to Billie Fountain

The computer screen blurred as I re-read her last words to me. There was to be a gathering of friends on October 7, her birthday. The time and menu were set. In her email reply she and Don promised to make the coffee. Before signing off, she wrote, "I can't wait!" in huge font.

Two days before her 86th birthday, Billie Fountain died at her beloved home. Heart failure. For a long time I stared at her words that night, facing the heart-wrenching realization that the anticipated celebration with this dear friend was not to be. Finally, the email message came back into focus, and my heart smiled through the tears, as I considered those final words, so typical of this amazing woman. "I can't wait!"

Billie had a way of bringing people into her life, making them feel special. At the same time she fondly shared bits of her past, and listeners felt her contentment. She was born in Tahona, Oklahoma, a coal miner's daughter, the youngest of six children. Times were hard. The Bunch family moved to other mining towns, eventually settling in Colorado. It was in Denver that Billie met and married young Don Fountain, Airman First Class. Together they embraced life for more than 65 years. The couple lived on bases in California and Washington. Two daughters and a son joined their Air Force family, and soon military life led them overseas where they reveled in new experiences, and Billie honed her taste for Victorian style. After living in England for four years, the Fountain family moved to Missouri Valley for the next lively chapter, as the children grew to adulthood.

A love of literature, a talent for entertaining, and a desire to add joy to people's lives blended together to form the perfect volunteer. Billie cheerfully greeted townspeople at the Rand Community Center where she set tables and assisted with meals for many years. She organized literary and holiday parties, uniting all age groups to produce memorable events that included food and fun. (I have yet to hear the stories of her legendary Halloween parties!) Billie happily wrote the scripts, cast the parts, and directed small theater events, complete with costumes, which she often provided. On the day of the "show" she sat in the back with a big smile but would not accept credit for her weeks of hard work.

Later, the woman devoted her talents to the public library, never fatiguing in her creativity. Jane Austen and the Bronte sisters were honored with choreographed pageants. Billie inspired children at the library to read Beatrix Potter and imitate her art. She created and donated themed treats for each child at the annual painting classes. When asked if she needed help, she replied as if singing, "No thank you. I've got it." Then she clasped her hands under her chin and her face beamed like the sun. "I can't wait!"

A mealtime invitation to the Fountain home meant royal treatment. Perfectly placed settings of Staffordshire china adorned a lovely, lace tablecloth. Scenes of colonial New England graced each plate. Matching cups and saucers were perfectly placed, and linen napkins were secured in coordinating china rings. The table overflowed with gourmet delights. Guests would sit gazing at the formal setting, thinking, "we should have dressed for the occasion!" The hostess would then sit, make us laugh with her dry wit, and two hours later, we found ourselves still at the table, still laughing, as we savored spoonfuls of her famous trifle.

Family was the heart of Billie Fountain's life. With profound gratitude, she spoke of their children, Pam, Kathy and Mark. Though the girls live far away, she said they stayed in close contact with the folks. Billie delighted in their frequent phone calls and emails. Visits were highly anticipated and celebrated. Mark and family often stopped in on weekends. Their loving mother joyfully regaled me of the family card games, the latest accomplishments, and of course, the "feast" that followed.

Love and pride was palpable every time Billie Fountain spoke of her grandsons, Greg and Jordan. Often her stories about their achievements began with her unforgettable "Oh! Dear! God!" She glowed with happiness and we knew her life was full and grand as she excitedly anticipated the next celebration.

As I write this, Billie's last words to me stream into brilliant focus. I can see this beloved wife, mother, grandmother and friend now as she strolls through the banquet halls of heaven. A brief consult with the head chefs confirms ample servings of butter at each table and real whipped cream topping the trifle. With a soft laugh, she adds, "Hey, at least we don't have to worry about cholesterol up here!"

A round of uncontrollable laughter bursts from the group on the stage. She encourages the band of angels as they rehearse her latest skit written after conferring with Charlotte Bronte who shares Billie's philosophy, "Happiness quite unshared can scarcely be called happiness."

Walking among the tables, she lovingly smooths a soft linen napkin and tucks it closer to the china plate. She gazes at the magnificence spread out before her, anticipating the glorious feast to come. At last, she clasps her hands tightly under her chin and squeezes her eyes shut. Then, face beaming like the sun, she whispers, "I can't wait!"

(Photo by Barbara Magill)

ABOUT THE AUTHOR

DeAnn (Wolkow) Kruempel was born and raised on a farm near De Smet, South Dakota. She has also lived in rural North Dakota and Iowa. For more than 30 years she has worked at school and public libraries

The author enjoys working in her orchard, reading and spending time with family and friends. She lives on an acreage near Logan, Iowa with her cat, Elsa, 9433 honeybees, four ducks and 16 chickens.

Besides her six published books, *Promises to Keep, Promises Challenged, Promises Strengthened, Promises in Courage,* and *Promises Under Fire,* and *Once Upon a Midwest Sunset* (available at Amazon.com), DeAnn Kruempel currently writes a column, PUTTING ON THE BIG BOOTS, that appears in three Midwest newspapers, *The Kingsbury Journal, The Missouri Valley Times-News* and *The Platte Enterprise.*

CREDITS and THANKS

Thanks for the memories!

Many ideas and stories in these essays come from my family. Often, I call or text one of my siblings: "What do you remember about....?" They always respond. I am so thankful to have them and I love reminiscing.

Many thanks to Dorothy and Bruce who edit stories every week.

Thanks to Nathan at BookStudio for your excellent work in publishing.

Thank you, readers, for your positive feedback. Knowing that a story evokes special memories for you makes writing worthwhile!

My siblings (and spouses) in Delmer's back yard. Darlene, Ted, Judy, Ed, Dorothy, Deloris, Delmer.

www.ingramcontent.com/pod-product-compliance
Lightning Source LLC
Chambersburg PA
CBHW081149090426
42736CB00017B/3252